DISPOSITIONS AS HABITS OF MIND

Making Professional Conduct More Intelligent

Erskine S. Dottin

D1596945

University Press of America,® Inc.
Lanham · Boulder · New York · Toronto · Plymouth, UK

Copyright © 2010 by
University Press of America,® Inc.
4501 Forbes Boulevard
Suite 200
Lanham, Maryland 20706
UPA Acquisitions Department (301) 459-3366

Estover Road
Plymouth PL6 7PY
United Kingdom

Library of Congress Control Number: 2009938682
ISBN: 978-0-7618-4963-6 (paperback : alk. paper)
eISBN: 978-0-7618-4964-3

TO

My friends (my students, university and public school colleagues) who are my chosen family.

CONTENTS

FOREWORD

As far back as I can remember I could never pinpoint the reasons behind some of the stuff that I did, and do up to now. Usually you do something with a good reason; an ulterior motive perhaps, or because you are motivated by uncertain incentive. But I think that I can chalk it up to just being curious about the outcome of my actions, without really considering the consequences, which were usually adverse in nature (being grounded, being spanked, reprimanded somehow, etc.). But like they say, hindsight is 20/20 indeed. One definitely sees the consequences, long-term and short-term, of one's actions. Upon doing something, like taking a certain action, certain consequences affect how I would do it differently, or if I would do the same thing altogether. But I don't think that I was ever really taught to fall into that rut. After a while, I could almost call it a reflex, or a habit. You know, my father (the author of this book) always tried to get me into the habit of asking why (I'm probably thinking "why ask why"), to actually penetrate to the core reason of an action and see if the expected end result would be something of use to everyone, or if it was more appealing to self; eventually I got to see that myself and that "why" shows a consideration for all parties involved. Mother, whose diligence through reading was evident in damn near everything she does, always expressed the need to be thorough. Whether it be the most simple detail, or the very elaborate of assignments, the ability to scrutinize something is a valuable trait as well as a good habit to have. I recall throughout my K-12 schooling, I was always cutting corners. Yeah, I cut corners like they were unnecessary, but when it came to who was checking my schoolwork, I was always hoping to win the war of attrition against my mother. I would go to her repeated times with the schoolwork finished, not caring about the outcome of whether every question was right or not. My thought was, if I made her check it over and over, she would finally let me off the hook. But of course, bulldogs never let their victims go either. It would usually be at the expense of a couple hours of sleep or a couple hours of playtime, both of which I always looked forward to after my homework, like any kid would. But I'm probably like most children when I say that getting everything right the first time wasn't priority one! At that time, I entertained the thought of scrutiny, not evaluating that the final result would probably net me more free time to do what I wanted rather than using that spare time to have to correct my mistakes. I chalk that up now to just trying to be a normal kid, not a perfectionist.

But being a perfectionist is not all that bad. In fact, in my current job as an Air Force Airman, *Excellence in All We Do* is one of our core values. But can we call excellence a habit really? Websters' defines EXCELLENCE as "The quality of being excellent; state of possessing good qualities in an eminent degree; exalted merit; superiority in virtue." No, the habit of unwavering scrutiny and attention to detail most often yields the favorable result of excellence. So excellence is the intended goal from having a habit to scrutinize. The most basic of principles of our basic military training is to pay strict attention to detail in anything we do. We miss a string on our uniform, it is a demerit. You miss a word of a creed, it is wrong. You miss a bolt on an F-15 Strike Eagle, and you may cost the pilot of that airframe his or her life, let alone cause irreparable damage to a multi-million dollar aircraft. Another good habit that is encouraged to the utmost is to apply precedent and experience to a situation that may not have been encountered before. Be it Enlisted or Officer, a quality leader among leaders will exhibit the talent of being able to apply one's experiences to a problem or situation. This will always give way to a person who will be able to think on his toes, and will expand his or her subordinate's ability to come up with unique answers to common issues. Now consider this for a second, because this is common to all branches of the military and not just the Air Force. Let us take a group of personnel in an office who are presented with a unique task with a very close suspense date. The supervisor of these personnel lays out the details of this task to everyone. Let us say that the supervisor has not seen any of these elements before. Sometimes it is hard for someone to make a connection with a present problem, and a situation that they have experienced that shows similarities. This person, to try to help the group, should share these experiences to try to turn the wheels of the collective and grind out a solution set to properly get things done. This is all assuming that the personnel in this office are all trained individuals in their field, and the assignment is not something that is above their skill set. Conversely, let's say that the supervisor has experienced something similar to the task presented, but does not try to make a connection between the prior experiences' solution, and the task, thus making it harder to tailor a solution from scratch. Remember that there was a suspense as well, so the former situation of lending the knowledge of prior experiences to others is the favorable habit to have. Who could benefit more from learning about the habits of the mind than the United States Military? In my opinion, for a leader to understand his decisions and to give proper orders that benefit the force as a whole, he must be able to identify with these habits to mentally charge his or her decisions and actions.

But why limit habits of mind to just educators and military service members? This is something applicable to professionals as a whole. Professionals constantly base day to day decisions, actions, thought patterns, etc. on very critical and specific patterns of thought. And, depending on the outcome, these patterns of thought are committed to a routine, or habits.

To understand these habits will most likely sharpen a person's ability to think of solutions subjectively, apply knowledge from an experience perspective, and emphasize giving and receiving quality feedback to further improve decisions and actions.

Farrell Sylvester Dottin, Senior Airman, United States Air Force

PREFACE

This work is a manifestation of the continued educational journey of the author. If John Dewey is correct that "education is the continued capacity for growth" then my reflections on my earlier experiences with "dispositions" has yielded clearer meaning for me with regard to dispositions as habits of mind that render professional conduct in education more intelligent. This clearer meaning is being transferred to and through this book.

At the forefront of my educational journey have been the salient and poignant words of Ron Ritchhart:

> What if education were less about acquiring skills and knowledge and more about cultivating the dispositions and habits of mind that students will need for a lifetime of learning, problem solving, and decision making? What if education were less concerned with the end-of-year exam and more concerned with who students become as a result of their schooling? What if we viewed smartness as a goal that students can work toward rather than as something they either have or don't? Reenvisioning education in this way implies that we will need to rethink many of our well-accepted methods of instruction. We will need to look beyond schools as training grounds for the memory and focus more on schooling as an enculturative process that cultivates dispositions of thinking"
> Ron Ritchhart, (2002) *Intellectual Character, p.* xxii

s (the teacher education candidates in my
lations of education course in summer 2009)
who have contributed to my educational
wledge my professional colleagues on the
AM-C) Task Force of the American Asso-
ACTE) for sharing their intellectual acumen

INTRODUCTION

Enhancing dispositions in teacher education and other professional school personnel candidates has been given great significance in the United States of America in the accreditation standards of the National Council for Accreditation of Teacher Education (NCATE) (2002), and the standards of the Interstate New Teacher Assessment and Support Consortium (INTASC) (1992), and in the work, among others, of Diez and Raths ((2007) Koeppen and Davison-Jenkins (2007), Sockett (2006), and Katz and Raths (1984).

However, it is clear from the literature that educators are just beginning to grapple with the definitional and philosophical aspects of the construct. I make this point in my article, "Professional Judgment and Dispositions in Teacher Education," published January 2009 in *Teaching and Teacher Education, Volume 25, Issue 1, 83-88.* In that work, I note how Larry Freeman (2007) highlights alternative terms being used for "dispositions": (a) temperament, (b) traits, and (c) habits, and point out that this lack of consensus regarding a clear definition of dispositions is further compounded by those educators who construe professional action as simply what Biesta (2007) calls "educational practice as intervention." In this context, teaching and learning is filtered through a medical model, in which students are made analogous to patients to be cured, and, as such, the knowledge from research that provides the most effective means for the cure, serves as the dominant paradigm for professional practice. Biesta (2007) contends that when professional action is viewed as effective intervention, then professional action: "is based [simply] on the idea that professionals do something -- they administer a treatment, they intervene in a particular situation – in order to bring about certain effects" (p. 7). Effective professional action in this context centers on "the quality of processes," and eschews the salient concern vis-à-vis "effective for what purpose." An example of the foregoing may be gleaned from the call by Wilkerson (2005) to eschew the moral in the understanding and assessment of teacher dispositions, and instead focus on asking students about their teachers, and then deduce the teacher's dispositions based on those student responses.

But, to shun purpose in professional action separates means and end, and as Biesta (2007) notes, to do so would presuppose that "the ends of professional action are given, and that the only relevant (professional and research) questions to be asked are about the most effective and efficient ways of achieving those ends" (p. 8). In this situation, technical means triumph over normative ends. But, "knowledge about the effectiveness of interventions is not, as such, a sufficient basis for decisions about educational action.

There is always the question as to whether particular interventions are *desirable*" (Biesta, 2007, p. 9). Professional action should, therefore, presuppose judgment about not only "what is possible," but "what is educationally desirable" (Biesta, 2007).

What is desirable in any teacher education program, whether in the United States or internationally should be linked to the salient question of what one is trying to foster in teacher education candidates. On the other hand, the question of what one is trying to foster presupposes a sense of purpose. However, to have a sense of purpose brings to the fore "moral agency," that is, purpose directing conduct, and providing justification for why one's purpose is good (Dewey, 1960).

Purpose is formulated through ends. As a result, for example, if the aim of education is to facilitate "the continued capacity for growth" in a democratic society (Dewey, 1944) then developing and nurturing dispositions for democratic ends should be consistent with the means of moral inquiry as advanced by Dewey (1922, 1938, 1944) and Misco and Shiveley (2007). On the other hand, if as Sockett (2006) maintains that education is about the development of intellectual virtues then dispositional ends would be consistent with moral virtues as advocated by Aristotle (Spangler, 1998). Conversely, if as Wasicsko (2007) views education as self-development then dispositional ends would be consistent with perceptual characteristics.

In fact, Misco and Shiveley (2007) reviewed statements about dispositions in teacher education programs across the United States of America and concluded that the use of the term "disposition" in these programs could be collapsed into three different categorical aims: (a) dispositions as personal virtues, (b) dispositions as educational values, and (c) dispositions as societal transformation. These authors, however, point out the means-ends disconnect in many of these programs with regard to dispositions by noting that "Some of the dispositions contained within the three categories of personal virtues, educational values, and societal transformation are statements about ends, while others concern means" (Misco & Shiveley, 2007, para. 12). More importantly, Misco and Shiveley (2007) note that the use of dispositions in many of these programs "assume an end goal *a priori*" (para. 12). For example, some programs that focus on social justice as dispositions unconsciously assume *a priori* ends with regard to "distributive problems of societal goods" (Misco & Shiveley, 2007, para. 26).

But, to assume *a priori* ends neglects the relevance of reflective intelligence in means-ends connections. As Dewey (1933, 1944) argues, means and ends are reciprocally determined, and the salient ingredient in the reciprocity is the kind of practical judgment required in problematic situations that require deliberation. In this context, "dispositions can effectively arise as habits when [professional educator candidates] have consistent exposure to certain kinds of learning experiences [deliberative] in their programs" (Misco & Shiveley, 2007, para. 14).

The constant in deliberative experiences, according to Dewey (1944) is "inquiry." Consequently, dispositions as habits of mind for inquiry require reflective intelligence, and reflective intelligence enhances professional judgment if reflective intelligence is associated with enabling educators to increase their capacity to solve pedagogical problems, make informed pedagogical decisions, and generate new knowledge in the world of practice (Osterman & Kottkamp, 2004).

So, is the conversation about dispositions in teacher education (Smith, Skarbek & Hurst, 2005) not really a conversation about professional conduct, and thus about making that professional conduct more intelligent? If so, then professional conduct would presuppose good judgment. But, professional judgment is linked to educational purpose, and having a sense of purpose brings to the fore moral agency, and reinforces the idea that purpose is formulated through ends, and that means-ends are determined reciprocally, the ingredient in this reciprocity being that practical judgment required in problematic situations requires deliberation.

This work seeks to assist the field of teacher education, both in the USA and internationally in gaining a better understanding of "dispositions," and, at the same time to offer working connections between professional judgment and dispositions, and provide grounding for the construct as "habits of mind" that render professional conduct more intelligent.

CHAPTER ONE

DISPOSITIONS AS ACTIVE MEANS - HABITS

John Dewey (1922) brings to our attention that, in many instances, references to the term "habit" is usually associated with the idea of bad habits such as gambling and addiction. In that context, habits are perceived as an internal mechanism that makes us act in some way and, in the case of "bad habits" in some way of which we are ashamed. Dewey (1922), however, contends that habits are means waiting, like tools in a box, to be used by conscious resolve. For example, nails and boards by themselves may be seen simply as materials, and a hammer and a saw as tools. The materials and tools do nothing by themselves. However, when a person brings to bear the aim to build a box, that is, to act with meaning, he/she has an end in view, and the materials and tools now become actual means toward that end. The individual brings bodily and mental organs into organization with external materials and tools in order to accomplish definite results. Dewey (1922) refers to these organizations as "habits." Habits are thus the connection between ends (what is to be done) and means (how it is to be done).

But, the aim to build the box does not arrive as a given, but out of human experience in the world. There is a behavioral view of human conduct that rests on the idea that the human organism is always at a state of rest, and moves only to satisfy drives, needs, etc. (Anderson, 2008). To the contrary is Dewey's view that children do not start with ends in view (an aim), but they are constantly in motion in experiencing the world through impulsive action. To Dewey (as cited in Anderson, 2008), "ends in view arise from the child's experiences of the consequences of its impulsive activity" (para.6). The child's impulses "demand some outlet for their expression, but what ends they eventually seek depends on the environment, especially on others' responses to the child" (Anderson, 2008, para. 6).

To illustrate:

> A newborn infant cries when it is hungry, at first with no end in view. It observes that crying results in a feeding, which relieves its hunger. It gets the idea that by crying, it can get relief. When crying is prompted by this idea, the child sees it as a means to a further end, and acts for the first time on a desire (that is, with an end in view). What desires the child ends up having are critically shaped by others' responses to its original impulsive,

activity, by the results that others permit crying to achieve. Parents who respond indis-
criminately to their children's crying end up with spoiled children whose desires expand
and proliferate without consideration for the interests of others. Parents who respond se-
lectively shape not only their children's use of means (crying) but also their ends, which
are modulated in response to the resistance and claims of others. This plasticity of ends as
well as means is possible because the original motor source of the child's activity is impulse not desire. Impulses demand some outlet for their expression, but what ends they
eventually seek depends on the environment, especially on others' responses to the child
(Anderson, 2008, para. 6).

So, acting on the world and undergoing the consequences generates ideas which, in
turn, may be used as a means to achieve some new end in view. Applying the means to
achieve the end is affected by the environment and thus, in turn, means and ends are determined reciprocally. This means – ends connection facilitates learning from experience.
According to Dewey (1916/1944), to learn from experience, and thus grow, means:

the power to retain from one experience something which is of avail in coping with the
difficulties of a later situation. This means power to modify actions on the basis of the results of prior experiences, the power to *develop dispositions*. Without it, the acquisition of
habits is impossible (p. 44).

Dispositions modify our actions on the basis of results of prior experiences. "In learning one act, methods are developed good for use in other situations....The human being
acquires a habit of learning. He learns to learn" (Dewey, 1916/1944, p. 45). Dispositions
as habits may be seen as expressions of growth.

plasticity is the capacity to retain and carry over from prior experience factors which
modify subsequent activities. This signifies the capacity to acquire habits, or develop
definite dispositions . . . a habit is a form of executive skill, of efficiency of doing. A
habit means an ability to use natural conditions as means to ends. It is an active control of
the environment through control of the organs of action (Dewey, 1916/1944, p. 46).

Hansen (2002) notes that "To retain the ability to learn from experience obliges a person to cultivate, among other things, what Dewey calls, 'personal attitudes' toward thinking and acting in the world. These attitudes include...straightforwardness, open-
mindedness, breadth of outlook, integrity of purpose, and responsibility. Such qualities
characterize a person who is extending and deepening an interest in learning from all of
his or her contacts in the world, whether the latter be weighty or light, momentary or en-
during, pleasant or trying" (p. 269). Hansen (2002) interprets Dewey's view of this extending and deepening interest in learning from experience as "the essential moral interest." Hansen (2002) says it is "moral . . . because it pivots around ongoing, responsive
engagement with other human beings and their projects, purposes, and hopes . . . [and] it
is essential because it is vital, significant, and decisive for the direction human life can

take. . . . Such interest fuels the possibility of a flourishing life for individual and society alike (p. 269).

If education is the process of forming dispositions – intellectual and emotional – toward nature and fellowmen then teachers should play a central role in helping students develop the essential moral interest – through educative environments (Hansen, 2002, p. 269).

But, let us return, for a moment, to our earlier dialogue about the nails and boards (materials), the hammer and saw (tools), and the person bringing to bear the aim to build a box. It was noted that the individual brings bodily and mental organs into organization with the external materials and tools so as to accomplish definite results. If according to Dewey (1916/1944) "a habit is a form of executive skill, of efficiency in doing. A habit means an ability to use natural conditions as means to ends" (p. 46), then one may easily see that changes in the natural conditions call forth the necessary habit(s). If changes in the natural conditions are such that box building is inhibited in any way, then the ability to summons the habit of "persisting" is critical to accomplishing definite results. In this instance, "Knowledge of methods alone will not suffice; there must be the desire, the will to employ them. This desire is an affair of personal disposition" (Dewey, 1933, p. 30).

Dewey (1916/1944) illuminates this point accordingly:

> savages react to a flaming comet as they are accustomed to react to other events which threaten the security of their life. Since they try to frighten wild animals or their enemies by shrieks, beating of gongs, brandishing of weapons, etc., they use the same methods to scare away the comet. To us, the method is plainly absurd – so absurd that we fail to note that savages are simply falling back upon habit in a way which exhibits its limitations . . . a habit apart from knowledge supplies us with a single fixed method of attack, knowledge means that selection may be made from a much wider range of habits (p. 340).

Katz and Raths (1985) embed the foregoing thinking in teacher education by calling for attention in programs to teacher dispositions whereby educators might gain a better understanding of teachers' actions in particular contexts, that is, their mastery of a skill, and the related pattern of employing the skill. The acquisition of the skill does not automatically guarantee the employment of the skill.

So, in teacher education programs candidates acquire knowledge and skills to enable them to act/conduct themselves in classrooms. But if conditions in the classroom change, classroom change, as in the example of building the box, then teacher education candidates must have the necessary dispositions: be aware of the need to change; have the necessary inclination to change, and engage in the necessary reflective activity to enhance change (Ritchhart, 2002).

If Chambliss (1987) is correct that "Education involves courses of action in which teachers aim to act together with their students to bring about certain conditions" (p. 1) then habituation must be transcended in order for both teachers and students to grow; the ability to change practice is contingent upon "habits as expressions of growth" (Dewey, 1916/1944, p. 46), "habits which transform the environment" (Dewey, 1916/1944, p. 48).

> Active habits involve thought, invention, and initiative in applying capacities to new aims. They are opposed to routine which marks an arrest of growth. Since growth is the characteristic of life, education is all one with growing; it has no end beyond itself. The criterion of the value of school education is the extent in which it creates a desire for continued growth and supplies means for making the desire effective in fact (Dewey, 1916/1944, pp. 52-53).

To enhance teacher education candidates' growth, teacher educators must not only assist teacher education candidates to acquire knowledge and skills, but must also help them develop their dispositions as teachers: their awareness of, inclinations, and reflections related to their thinking and actions (Ritchhart, 2002).

A disposition, in teaching and learning, may be defined as a tendency toward a general type of action in pedagogical situations; the teacher and learner tending to approach situations in a certain way and displaying a general set of actions associated with the disposition. Pedagogical dispositions should lead to better and more powerful pedagogy.

Active Means Waiting to be Used

So acting on the world experientially leads to the formation of related habits, whether positively or negatively. These habits formed are active means awaiting use for some end(s). These active means may be construed of as the internal motivation of a set of actions and responses to the world (Dewey, 1933; Ritchhart, 2002). These habits (or dispositions) "do not cause us to do anything. Our actions stem from our cognitive appraisals of situations in which we must act within which our dispositions are embedded" (Dottin, 2009, p. 85). For example, at the start of my education courses, I ask candidates to engage in the following activity. First, I ask them to reflect on their prior experience(s) in taking classes, and list ideas that come to mind based on their experience(s) in their taking classes as students. I then ask candidates to identify habits they have formed that are related to their experience(s) in taking classes. Finally, I ask them to provide evidence of their behavior in a recent class situation that was subconsciously based on the habits formed. I then show candidates how these habits are active means in terms of their waiting to be used in my class situation. If they have formed habits of approaching things in the way to which they have become accustomed, and my course requires a new or different approach then their behavior might be that of complaining about their not having ever experienced any such approach and therefore behaving in ways that show that they do not like the situation. Carver and Enfield (2006) state "people develop habits of emotional response, perceptions, appreciation, sensitivity, and attitude. These habits developed from past experiences, affect future experiences" (pp. 56-57).

Since the candidates' prior experiences were acquired in social contexts, and situations, then one may infer that "Habits are socially shaped dispositions to particular forms of activity or modes of responses to the environment. They channel impulses in specified directions, toward certain outcomes, by entrenching particular uses of means, prescribing certain conduct in particular circumstances" (Anderson, 2008, para. 7).

Furthermore, as noted by John Dewey (1922), since habits operate subconsciously then they cannot be changed simply by willing them to change.

> While habits incorporate purposes and socially meaningful ideas, they operate beneath the actor's consciousness. Once people have learned how to achieve some purpose and entrenched that mode of conduct in a habit or skill, they no longer need to tend to what they are doing in achieving it. Such tending may even interfere with successful performance. Habits by receding from awareness, conserve people's reflective resources, make their activity fluid, and enable them to reliably produce certain results (provided the environment remains the same) (Anderson, 2008, para. 8).

According to Dewey (as cited in Anderson, 2008) "when habits are blocked, people are forced to stop their activity and reflect on the problems posed by the situation; they must deliberate, that is, they must engage in intelligent conduct" (para. 11), in other words, they must engage in reflective appraisal of their conduct. When they do, the dispositions of intelligent conduct become habits (active means such as questioning, thinking, being open-minded, managing impulsivity, and so on). Support for the foregoing proposition also comes from the social theory of symbolic interactionism (Blumer, 1969;): "Action follows the course of habit until encountering a blockage that in turn triggers an impulse that conflicts with the habit. Intelligence arbitrates between habit and impulse, thereby securing the release of action" (Reynolds 1993, p. 26).

Habits and Teacher Conduct

The current work on teacher dispositions highlights the serious effort to help teachers and other professional school personnel to form habits and use them as active means in making their professional conduct more effective, that is, more intelligent. Some label this effort as enhancing teaching effectiveness (Knopp & Smith, 2005), and teacher excellence (Collinson, 1999); some as enhancing teacher affect (Wilkerson & Lang, 2007); others as enhancing the teacher as person (Wasicsko, 2007); and as enhancing moral conduct (Sockett, 2006; Osguthorpe, 2008; Burant, Chubbuck & Whipp, 2007); and still others as enhancing professional judgment (Dottin, 2009).

CHAPTER TWO

MAKING PROFESSIONAL CONDUCT MORE EFFECTIVE

The use of the term "dispositions" in the current educational literature is based on the effort to move beyond what teachers (and other school professionals) know (their knowledge), and what they can do (their ability), to what they are actually likely to do with that knowledge and ability. The question "can you play the guitar?" is a question about one's knowledge and skills. The question "do you play the guitar?" is a question about one's inclination, one's disposition (Ritchhart, 2002). The link between pedagogical ability (knowledge and skills), and the deployment of that ability is what is being referred to in the literature as "dispositions." It may be conceptualized as the consistent internal motivation to act, and as in the case of teaching and learning, to act with professional judgment. Dottin (2009) notes that "knowledge and skills, utilized by professional educators in educational settings, are influenced [or most definitely should be influenced] by the consistent internal motivation for them to conduct themselves intelligently or, in other words, to exercise sound professional judgment in action" (p. 85). That consistent internal motivation may also be captured conceptually as "habit" to express the underlying motivator and organizer of intelligent behavior.

Davis (1992) notes that professionals offer, and are expected to deliver competent judgment. In fact, "an engineer without engineering judgment, a lawyer without a lawyer's judgment, or any other professional without the particular form of judgment distinguishing his or her profession from all others, would be an incompetent 'layman' who could not honestly practice the profession in question" (Davis, 1992, para. 1).

Some scholars have concluded that teaching is a professional practice that requires both theoretical and practical judgment (Coulter, et al., 2007). These scholars maintain that knowing what to do in teaching is not enough, that teachers must act, and to act requires practical judgment: "which involves doing the right thing at the right time for the right reasons with the right people, and thus its importance for teaching" (Coulter, et al., 2007, para. 15).

The work of Fuller (1969) has brought to the fore a developmental conceptualization of teachers that adds to better understanding teaching and professional judgment. On the one hand, this work noted that beginning professionals are consumed with achieving technical competence and, therefore, focus exclusively on survival concerns such as adequacy, control, being liked and, consequently, do not demonstrate habits of reflective practice. On the other hand, this work has also indicated that experienced teachers showed less concern for technical competence, and demonstrated more habits of reflective practice, the basis of practical judgment.

In his book, *Qualities of Effective Teachers*, James H. Stronge (2002) while not using the concept of habits or dispositions concludes that one of the vital aspects of effective teachers is their personal characteristics: "Studies suggest that instructional and management processes are key to effectiveness, but many interview and survey responses about effective teaching emphasize the teacher's affective characteristics, or social and emotional behaviors, more than pedagogical practice" (p.13). One of these affective characteristics, according to Stronge (2002) is "the role of reflective practice" (p. 20). This affective characteristic of reflective practice, like the others identified by Stronge (2002)– caring, listening, understanding, respecting, social awareness, and passion for learning– moves the discussion of effective teachers beyond what teachers know (their knowledge), and what they can do (their ability), to what they are actually likely to do with that knowledge and ability, their dispositions.

Dewey (as cited in Anderson, 2008) suggests that there are 3 levels of conduct: impulse, habit, and reflective action. The survival conduct exhibited by beginning teachers, as described by Fuller (1969) may be seen as analogous to impulse, and the reflective action of experienced and effective teachers as reflective conduct. The effort of teacher education programs is to help candidates move, like children, past impulse to the more intelligent level of pedagogical conduct, that is, to grow in professional judgment. But, to do so requires the understanding that impulsive conduct: "… can be directed and shaped toward various ends. Children's primitive impulses to move their bodies energetically can be directed through education, toward the development of socially valued skills and interpersonally coordinated activity" (Anderson, 2008, para. 5).

Dewey's concept of "plasticity," that is, the ability to learn from experience, links the levels of impulse and habit. To repeat an earlier quote helps here:

> A newborn infant cries when it is hungry, at first with no end in view. It observes that crying results in a feeding, which relieves its hunger. It gets the idea that by crying, it can get relief. When crying is prompted by this idea, the child sees it as a means to a further end, and acts for the first time on a desire (that is, with an end in view). What desires the child ends up having are critically shaped by others' responses to its original impulsive activity, by the results that others permit crying to achieve. Parents who respond indiscriminately to their children's crying end up with spoiled children whose desires expand and proliferate without consideration for the interest of others. Parents who respond se-

lectively shape not only their children's use of means (crying) but also their ends, which are modulated in response to the resistance and claims of others. This plasticity of ends as well as means is possible because the original motor source of the child's activity is impulse, not desire. Impulses demand some outlet for their expression, but what ends they eventually seek depends on the environment, especially others' responses to the child (Anderson, 2008, para. 6).

So, habits are formed, whether positively or negatively, as one learns from experience. "Habits are socially shaped dispositions to particular forms of activity or modes of response to the environment. They channel impulse in specified directions, toward certain outcomes, by entrenching particular uses of means, prescribing certain conduct in particular circumstances" (Anderson, 2008, para. 7). An example of the foregoing may be gleaned from our acquisition of "taste" as a shared habit of a group. "A young child just starting out on solid food may be open to eating anything. But every society limits what it counts as edible. Certain foods become freighted with social meaning–as suitable for celebrating birthdays, good for serving to guests,....The child's hunger becomes refined into a taste [a disposition/habit] for certain foods on particular occasions" (Anderson, 2008, para. 7).

Habits, however, operate subconsciously: "Once people have learned how to achieve some purpose and entrenched that mode of conduct in a habit or skill, they no longer need to tend to what they are doing in achieving it" (Anderson, 2008, para. 8). More importantly, habits "entrench modes of conduct rather than ends in view [so] when the environment changes, they may produce different results than originally intended" (Anderson, 2008, para. 9). Changing habits cannot be done by willing change (Dewey, 1922), changing habits can only be achieved by grasping the means that can bring about the change. In other words, "We must resort to indirect means, especially alteration of the environment to check an unsatisfactory habit" (Anderson, 2008, para. 9).

Habits, therefore, cannot be changed by willpower, but instead must be changed by "forms of education that instill habits of independent thought, critical inquiry, observation, experimentation, foresight, and imagination, including sympathy with others. Such an education can make habits themselves more flexible and responsive to changes in the context and consequences of conduct. It enables habits to incorporate intelligence" (Anderson, 2008, para. 10).

Dispositions of intelligent conduct (thinking, being open-minded, managing impulsivity, and so on) therefore, only become habits when social environments enhance persons engaging in deliberative inquiry.

The need to reflect intelligently on what one is doing arises when the ordinary operation of behavior or impulse is blocked.... When habit is blocked, people are forced to stop their activity and reflect on the problems posed by their situation. They must deliberate. The aim of deliberation is to find a satisfactory means to resumption of activity by solving the problem posed by one's situation. Deliberation involves an investigation of the causes of disrupted activity so as to consciously articulate the problematic features of one's situation, and an imaginative rehearsal of alterative means to solving it, anticipating the consequences of executing each one, including one's attitudes to those consequences. It is a thought experiment designed to arrive at a practical judgment, action upon which is anticipated to resolve one's predicament. Deliberation is more intelligent, the more articulate the definition of one's problem in light of more observant uptake of its relevant features, the more imaginative one is in coming up with feasible solutions, the more comprehensive and accurate one's views of the consequences of implementing them, and the more responsive is one's decision to its anticipated consequences, relative to the consequences of alternatives. Action on the practical judgments that proceed from deliberation is self-aware. As the individual gets more practice in intelligent conduct, the dispositions that make it up become habits (Anderson, 2008, para. 11).

In the foregoing context, "dispositions can effectively arise as habits when [professional educator candidates] have consistent exposure to certain kinds of learning experiences [deliberative] in their programs" (Misco & Shiveley, 2007, para. 14). The constant in deliberative experiences, according to Dewey (1944) is "inquiry." Consequently, dispositions as habits of mind for inquiry require reflective intelligence, and reflective intelligence enhances professional judgment if reflective intelligence is associated with enabling educators to increase their capacity to solve pedagogical problems, make informed pedagogical decisions, and generate new knowledge in the world of practice (Osterman & Kottkamp, 2004).

So, the qualities of effective teachers to which Stronge (2002) refers may be captured as "dispositions of pedagogical mindfulness and thoughtfulness (reflective capacity) that render professional educators' action and conduct more intelligent" (Dottin, 2009, p. 85). These habits of pedagogical mindfulness and thoughtfulness mean that pedagogues have a disposition toward enhancing the educational growth of all learners through the application of their thinking to things already known (content, process skills) for the purpose of improving social conditions. This requires that pedagogues demonstrate commitments to patterns of intellectual activity that guide their cognitive and social behavior in educational settings (with students, families, colleagues and communities) (Dottin, 2009; Dottin 2006).

If pedagogy is conceptualized as a goal-oriented, decision-making or problem solving process carried out in the interest of a client wherein the pedagogue gives reasoned consideration to relevant information, criteria, methods, context, principles, policies, and resources, then pedagogical dispositions represent characteristics that animate, motivate, and direct … abilities toward good and productive professional conduct and are recognized in the patterns of…frequently exhibited, voluntary behaviors. If the dispositions, that is, habits of mind, which in pedagogy are objects of intention, are to be distinguished from temperament, then they will have what may be termed a cognitive core. That is, pedagogical actions will stem from cognitive appraisals of situations in which the pedagogue must act and within which his/her dispositions are embedded.

So, what are the qualities of thought and affective characteristics that we can expect to see when someone is demonstrating pedagogical intelligence? According to Hansen (2001) cognitive connections made through the acquisition of information and of technical intellectual skill influences the formation of social dispositions.

In fact, Hansen (2001) contends that "The moral quality of knowledge lies not in its possession, but in how it can foster a widening consciousness and mindfulness. This moral cast of mind, embodies commitments to (i.e., habits of mind): straightforwardness, simplicity, naivete, open-mindedness, integrity of purpose, responsibility, and seriousness" (p. 59).

What qualities of thought does one expect to see when an educator is demonstrating intelligent professional conduct? Ritchhart (2002) suggests seeing the individual exhibiting the following: thinking creatively (being open-minded and curious); thinking reflectively (thinking about one's thinking); and thinking critically (seeking truth and understanding, being strategic, being skeptical).

Sockett (2006), on the other hand, expects to see: dispositions of character (self-knowledge, integrity–wisdom, courage, temperance, justice, persistence, and trustworthiness); dispositions of intellect (fairness and impartiality, open-mindedness, truthfulness, and accuracy); and dispositions of care (receptivity, relatedness, and responsiveness).

Costa & Kallick (2000) link the following to demonstrating intelligent professional conduct: persisting, managing impulsivity, listening with understanding and empathy, thinking flexibly, thinking about one's own thinking (metacognition), striving for accuracy, questioning and posing problems, applying past knowledge to new situations, thinking and communicating with clarity and precision, gathering data through all senses, creating, imagining, innovating, responding with wonderment and awe, taking responsible risks, thinking interdependently, finding humor, and remaining open to continuous learning.

Hansen (2001) relying on Dewey's idea of *How We Think* (1933), looks for evidence of intelligent professional conduct in the individual: being curious, open-minded, decisive, systematic, skeptical, deliberate, judicious, inquisitive, strategic, diligent, fair-minded, and reflective.

Barrell (1991), on the other hand, sees the characteristics of thoughtful persons [professionals] as suggested by research on teaching and cognitive development accordingly:

> They have confidence in problem solving abilities. They persist. They control their own impulsivity. They are open to others' ideas. They cooperate with others in solving problems. They listen. They are empathic. They tolerate ambiguity and complexity. They approach problems from a variety of perspectives. They research problems thoroughly. They relate prior experience to current problems and make multiple connections. They are open to many different solutions and evidence that may contradict favored points of view. They pose what-if questions, challenging assumptions and playing with variables. They are meta-cognitive: They plan, monitor, and evaluate their thinking. They are

able to transfer concepts and skills from one situation to another. They are curious and wonder about the world. They ask 'good questions (p. 34).

One may conclude that "...intelligent performance is not just an exercise of ability. It is more dispositional in nature in that we must activate...abilities and set them in motion. Dispositions concern not only what we can do, our abilities, but what we are actually likely to do, addressing the gap we often notice between our abilities and our actions" (Ritchhart, 2002, p. 18). Campbell (n.d.) contends that in the current global knowledge economy intelligent thinking behaviors are the key to self-regulated learning and life-long learning, and these intelligent thinking behaviors are habits of mind such as Thinking interdependently, Striving for Accuracy, Communicating with Clarity and Precision, and Taking Responsible Risks.

CHAPTER THREE

CULTIVATING DISPOSITIONS/HABITS OF MIND THROUGH MEANS OF INQUIRY

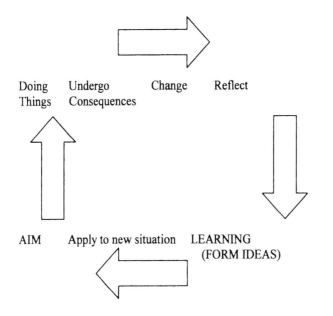

Doing   Undergo   Change   Reflect
Things   Consequences

AIM   Apply to new situation   LEARNING
                                 (FORM IDEAS)

"give the pupils something to do, not something to learn; and the doing is of such a nature as to demand thinking or the intentional noting of connections; learning naturally results" (Dewey, 1916/1944, p.154).

So, how is the consistent internal motivation to engage in pedagogical mindfulness and thoughtfulness cultivated and nurtured? Rather than seeing dispositions through a moral deontological framework of "conformity to the right," programs might focus on a moral stance of inquiry in which the reflective method of inquiry is given priority over fixed answers to questions about the good. Dewey (as cited in Anderson, 2008) suggests:

Individuals begin their lives as human societies did historically; acting on impulse and custom. These modes of conduct being unselfconscious and shortsighted cannot handle all the challenges life poses and generate problems of their own. Thus arises the need for reflective appraisal of conduct in view of its wider consequences with the aim of controlling future conduct by means of these appraisals so as to solve the problem at hand. This practical reasoning uses the same general experimental method as theoretical reasoning does. We begin with certain given facts; these are our immediate valuings of things by impulse and habit. The data for appraisal of these valuings come from the consequences of acting on them, along with the ways we value these consequences (para. 49).

To follow the above, programs would have to move from a "transmission model" of teaching in which the teacher just prepares and transmits information to learners, to an "enculturation model" in which the teacher creates a culture in the classroom in which the habits of mind, that is, dispositions that facilitate intelligent action and professional judgment are seen by candidates, are encouraged and orchestrated through candidate/candidate interaction, and are taught directly (Tishman, Jay and Perkins, 1992). This reinforces Dewey's notion that we never educate directly but by means of the environment (Dewey, 1916/1944). The environment, however, must be an "educative environment," which according to Hansen (2002) must be characterized by the following: (1) the environment must draw candidates into acting, and away from passive ingestion of information, (2) it must call out candidates' best thinking and not reinforce their biases, (3) it must help candidates pursue their own interests while interacting with others in ways that deepen social sympathies, and (4) it must help candidates see the interrelatedness of knowledge. The educative environment must enable candidates to acquire knowledge and skills in order to act.

Fostering habits or growing habits comes, therefore, from "doing" and reflecting on experience. To Dewey (1916/1944), experience is about trying and undergoing, and thus is the perception of the connection between something tried and something undergone (we suffer or enjoy the consequences); it is a process (activity) (p. 139).

It is not experience when a child merely sticks his finger into a flame; it is experience when the movement is connected with the pain which he undergoes in consequence. Henceforth the sticking of the finger into flame *means* a burn. Being burned is a mere physical change, like the burning of a stick of wood, if it is not perceived as a consequence of some other action (Dewey, 1916/1944, pp. 139-140).

The epistemological grounding for the idea that dispositions (i.e., habits of mind) are not a state of possession, but a state of performance is found in John Dewey's transactional theory of knowing (Biesta, 2007). According to Dewey, we undergo the consequences of our doing; our acting on the world and we change as a result. Experience results in change in the organic structures that conditions further behavior (Dewey, 1938). For example, the experience of eating includes what is experienced (the food), how it is experienced (through digestive system). We undergo the consequences (suffer or enjoy). We experience change. We connect our acts to the change and there is learning (the acquisition of meaning – ideas). Dewey refers to these changes as *habits*. Habits, then, are "not patterns of action, but predispositions to act" (Biesta, 2007, p. 14). In other words, "the essence of habits is an acquired predisposition to ways or modes of responses, not to particular acts .... Habit means special sensitiveness or accessibility to certain classes of stimuli, standing predilections and aversions, rather than bare recurrence of specific acts" (Dewey, 1922, p. 42).

We therefore acquire our habits through experimentation (we do, undergo the consequences of our doing, and change). Experimentation with deliberation and direction is intelligent action (thinking or reflection). We acquire new habits in those situations in which the organism-environment transaction is interrupted – we encounter a problem. Reflective experimental problem solving is consequently an inquiry process.

The power of reflective practice has increasingly moved to the forefront of the educational process (Mentkowski & Associates, 2000). Breese & Nawrocki-Chabin (2007) note that "We engage in some experience, some social interaction, some learning; but the full impact of that encounter for present learning and adaptation to future experience and problem solving remains incomplete unless we reflect on the how and why of that experience" (p. 36). Wong (2007) contends that:

> The degree that any activity is aesthetic and educative --- whether lifting a stone, creating art, or solving scientific problems --- is related to the degree that active doing and receptive undergoing are joined in perception. We do something, we undergo its consequences, we do something in response, we undergo again. And so on. The experience becomes educative as we grasp the relationship between doing and undergoing. The experience is transformative as we have new thoughts, feelings, and action, and also as the world reveals itself and acts upon us in new ways (para. 32).

But, on the one hand while many Colleges of Education in their conceptual frameworks and programs (Valli, 1992) and States in their standards for teachers and other school personnel readily identify reflection/inquiry as an appropriate standard (Rodgers, 2002), on the other hand, Spalding and Wilson (2002) contend that reflection remains a mysterious concept to many. These same authors note that while thinking is natural, habits consistent with reflective action must and should be taught in education, and they suggest that these habits would include being open-minded, exhibiting freedom from prejudice, and close mindedness, whole-heartedness, directness, curiosity, readiness and responsibility (Spalding and Wilson, 2002; Rodgers, 2002). They concur with Zeichner & Liston (1987) that "more reflective teacher actions will lead to greater benefits for the teacher and all of his or her pupils" (p. 25).

While Donald Schon (1983, 1987) is in the forefront with regard to the reflective practitioner, it is John Dewey (1933) who provides philosophical understanding vis-à-vis reflective thought. Dewey insists that to simply describe "the act" or "the situation" is not
reflection. Instead, reflection is to state the genuine possibility in the act or the situation.
Reflection thus requires that one weigh, ponder, or deliberate with regard to the act or
situation. Schubert (2005) extends our understanding here when he states that "Reflection
spurred by wonder, then, is a seed that transforms mere activity into experience" (p. 13).
To describe activity is not the same, therefore, as drawing reflective insights from activity. Rodgers (2002) identifies four criteria that characterize Dewey's idea of reflection:

> 1. Reflection is a meaning-making process that moves a learner from one experience into
> the next with deeper understanding of its relationships with and connections to other ex-
> periences and ideas. It is the thread that makes continuity of learning possible, and en-
> sures the progress of the individual and, ultimately, society. It is a means to essentially
> moral ends.
> 2. Reflection is a systematic, rigorous, disciplined way of thinking, with its roots in scien-
> tific inquiry.
> 3. Reflection needs to happen in community, in interaction with others.
> 4. Reflection requires attitudes that value the personal and intellectual growth of oneself
> and others (para. 12).

While Rodgers (2002) helps us see that reflection is a complex, rigorous, an intellectual endeavor, the same author also brings to the fore that reflective inquiry is guided by
certain habits of mind or habits consistent with reflective action., that is, with reflective
intelligence. Reflective intelligence may thus be construed as thinking back on what was
done in order to discover how one's actions may have contributed to an unexpected outcome (learning new ideas). However, to remain engaged in the foregoing experiential
process, while it is happening, necessitates the demonstration of reflective attitudes (dispositions) such as single-mindedness, directness, open-mindedness, responsibility (Rodgers, 2002).

Misco and Shiveley (2007) see deliberative inquiry as the best vehicle by and through
which teacher education programs may cultivate dispositions:

> Deliberation helps develop habits and attitudes consonant with educational values, de-
> mocratic virtues, and societal transformation in non-political ways. In the core of a meth-
> ods class and other program-specific courses, pre-service teachers can engage in delibera-
> tive approaches to work with colleagues, develop curriculum, solve problems, govern a
> classroom, and most prominently, as an instructional strategy. In all of these instances,
> deliberation can provide a process general enough for most any content area, yet firmly
> aligned with honoring the spirit of institutional, unit, and program area missions. Also,
> because deliberation is decidedly means-based, it is responsive to NCATE's dispositional
> charges in non-inculcative ways. When multiple program areas employ deliberation

throughout the curriculum, the resultant effect is a unit-wide conscious attempt to foster dispositions (para. 17.

To Misco & Shiveley (2007) "Rather than attempt the development of dispositions through transmission or direct instruction, dispositions can effectively arise as habits when pre-service teachers [educators] have consistent exposure to certain kinds of learning experiences in their programs" (para. 14). As a result, like Misco and Shiveley (2007) this author believes that the dispositions (the habits of mind for making professional conduct more intelligent) worthy of being nurtured in teacher education programs should have their roots within social reflective intelligence for democratic ends.

John Dewey maintains that "The business of the educator—whether parent or teacher—is to see to it that the greatest possible number of ideas acquired by children and youth are acquired in such a vital way that they become **moving** ideas, motive-forces in the guidance of conduct. This demand and this opportunity make the moral purpose universal and dominant in all instruction—whatsoever the topic" (Dewey, 2008, p. 10). So, the moral purpose of the school demands that instructional efforts to nurture habits of mind for transfer be guided by the aim "to bring intellectual results into vital union with character so that they become working forces in behavior" (Dewey, 2008, p. 11).

More importantly, Dewey (2008) argues that in so far as this pedagogical situation:

> represents, in its own spirit, a genuine community life; in so far as what are called school discipline, government, order, etc., are the expressions of this inherent social spirit; in so far as the methods used are those that appeal to the active and constructive powers, permitting the child to give out and thus to serve; in so far as the curriculum is so selected and organized as to provide the material for affording the child a consciousness of the world in which he has to play a part, and the demands he has to meet; so far as these ends are met, the school is organized on an ethical basis (p. 26).

Having professional educators participate in communities of practice in ways that make clear the knowledge, skills and habits of mind (dispositions) required for effective professionalism, and having them model those abilities for their candidates facilitates the process of transforming teacher education from a collection of courses to a moral developmental growth process. A key part of that growth process is helping candidates bring to a level of consciousness the connections between their intentions and actions (their habits of mind, i.e., their dispositions), the effectiveness of their decision-making, and their functioning within the larger community of learning, the profession (Diez, 2007).

Accordingly, working toward getting candidates and faculty members in professional education programs to demonstrate habits of mind through wisdom in practice is a moral endeavor in terms of doing the right thing at the right time for the right reason with the right people (Phelan, 2001; 2005), for "what is learned and employed in an occupation having an aim and involving cooperation with others is moral knowledge, whether consciously so regarded or not" (Dewey, 1944, p. 356).

The need to heed the call, by some, that building intellectual dispositions must be higher education's obligation (Broadbear, n.d.) takes on more urgency for teacher education programs in higher education institutions if teaching is seen through the lens of a clinical profession that requires discernment and judgment, problem-solving skills, continuous learning and the utilization of content knowledge to address problems.

On the other hand:

> The difference between mere knowledge, or information, and judgment is that the former is simply held, not used; judgment is knowledge directed with reference to the accomplishment of ends. Good judgment is a sense of respective or proportionate values. The one who has judgment is the one who has ability to size up a situation. He is the one who can grasp the scene or situation before him, ignoring what is irrelevant, or what for the time being is unimportant, who can seize upon the factors which demand attention, and grade them according to their respective claims (Dewey, 2008, p. 30).

So, to nurture habits of mind within a pedagogical context is to focus on the moral trinity of the school's demand for "social intelligence, social power, and social interests" (Dewey, 2008, p. 26). The foregoing is facilitated in "(1) the life of the school as a social institution itself; (2) methods of learning and of doing work; and (3) the school studies or curriculum" (Dewey, 2008, p. 26). More so, "The only way to prepare for social life is to engage in social life. To form habits of social usefulness and serviceableness apart from any direct social need and motive, apart from any existing social situation, is to the letter, teaching the child to swim by going through motions outside of the water" (Dewey, 2008, p. 15). The major theme in the foregoing is that "All education which develops power to share effectively in social life is moral" (Dewey, 1916/1944, p. 360).

Ritchhart (2002) suggests that dispositions can be nurtured and developed through the internalization of external triggers. These external triggers may come into play when the individual lacks the internal mechanisms, inclination, awareness or motivation to demonstrate a disposition. The kind of environment in which external triggers may be internalized (to bridge the gap between ability and action) is one in which candidates see the dispositions, they are taught about the dispositions, they practice demonstrating the dispositions, and there is consistency in the implicit messages sent by the teacher.

The process of building capacity for judgment in nurturing professional educators' habits of mind reinforces the call by dispositions assessment expert Mary Diez (2006): "The assessment of dispositions requires that teacher educators find a way to have candidates thoughtfully explore their reasoning and motivation and look at how they enact it through their words and actions" (p. 59). Such a process further assumes that the habits of mind which prevail are influenced by the thought of their bearing upon the development of candidates and faculty (Dewey, 1944, p. 19). The acquisition of habits of mind must be seen as the background of educational growth, and enlists the natural active tendencies of candidates in their doing something that requires observation, the acquisition of information, and the use of imagination.

The assessment of dispositions (the habits of mind that render professional conduct more intelligent) should, therefore, be approached as "building capacity for judgment" (Diez, 2007, p. 215). This approach attends to the "habits of heart" (desire for teaching) brought to programs by many teacher education candidates, and simultaneously fosters the more germane professional habits of mind that will render their conduct more intelligent (Sexton, 2008).

Albee and Piveral (2003) indicate that in order to assess the dispositional development of professional educators, the complex aspects of dispositions must be organized into an assessment instrument that assists professional educators in their identifying and monitoring the dispositions as well as a process by and through which they improve areas of concern. Koeppen & Davison-Jenkins (2007) reinforce this idea by getting candidates to observe, analyze, and judge their performance on the basis of public, explicit criteria and determine how to improve it (in campus classroom, in field, and world of practice) by utilizing a *Personal Qualitative Inventory.* Koeppen and Davison-Jenkins (2007) have candidates use written reflections to name and claim dispositions. Koeppen & Davison-Jenkins (2007) maintain that: Teacher educators need to purposely teach what dispositions are, for example, working through the various descriptors, providing concrete examples, and asking questions to stimulate critical thinking. We believe that the art of reflection lies somewhere within this process (p. 97).

Wasicsko, Callahan & Wirtz (n.d.) caution, however, that: Many institutions rely on student self-reflections to assess dispositions and their change over time. Behavioral checklists, observation reflections, journaling, and rating scale rubrics provide opportunities for self-assessment. These self-report approaches have proven valuable for a large number of teacher candidates. However, self-report instruments may not work well with individuals who cannot demonstrate the desired dispositions. Candidates who appear to be 'dispositional misfits' seem to be the most resistant to making accurate self-reflections that would lead to self-selecting out of programs, or to realistically see themselves as others perceive them. Combining student self-assessment with professional faculty judgment significantly increases the probability of obtaining valid data (p. 5).

Identifying, nurturing and assessing habits of mind in professional education programs presuppose that candidates will transfer their learning to the world of practice. Accordingly, working toward getting candidates, and faculty members in professional education program to demonstrate habits of mind through wisdom in practice is a moral endeavor in terms of doing the right thing at the right time for the right reason with the right people (Phelan, 2001; 2005), for "what is learned and employed in an occupation having an aim and involving cooperation with others is moral knowledge, whether consciously so regarded or not" (Dewey, 1944, p. 356).

If the capacity for judgment is enhanced in teacher education programs then "Patterns of action in preparation can be presumed to also show up later on the job. A candidate who demonstrates promptness, courtesy, etc. in his or her preparation will likely act similarly when on the job. Likewise, a person habitually rude, late, etc. in pre-service work will more than likely have trouble on the job ("Professional Dispositions Assessment [PDA] Form," 2006). In a field comparable to teaching, nursing, a study on first- and last-year nursing students in Finland examined the effects of ethics teaching on the development of moral judgment and found that students who had had to deal with ethical dilemmas in their practical training had higher moral judgment in practice than students who did not (Auvinen, Suominen, Leino-Kilpi, & Helkama, 2004).

Dispositions and their transfer might be gleaned from an example of the integrated learning curriculum that was taught in the Mt. Olive Township Public Schools in the United States. Habits of mind, such as, being thoughtful in actions, were fostered in daily classroom interactions between teachers and students, and students and students as follows: "...when a teacher [employed] 'wait time,' he or she [fostered] a management of impulsivity....When the teacher [asked] a question of the class and [told] them that she [did] not want an immediate response but rather [wanted] them to ponder the question, to have some time to think ("Thought-filled Learning Community," n.d.). More examples of the transfer of habits of mind, in which educators are rendering their professional conduct more intelligent may be seen in programs in Singapore, Australia, Canada, New Zealand, and Hong Kong ("Links," 2008).

Relevance of Inquiry

The relevance of inquiry may be gleaned by drawing contrasts between industrial age mass education, and 21st-century education:

> Industrial age, mass education focuses on compartmentalization, inputs and outputs, curricula and fields of study are broken down into digestible portions that teachers present to students whose task is to memorize and repeat the content back. Learning is framed as acquisition of known facts and information, teachers present questions that have ready answers and success is defined as being correct and fast....Education in the knowledge age, described by some as 21st century learning is characterized by ready access to ever expanding knowledge and to people around the globe. 21st century education requires that students and teachers engage directly with disciplinary problems, issues, questions and ideas, and with perspectives from around the world. 21st century learning requires that learners be engaged in meaningful and relevant knowledge building work using today's digital technologies. Sustained inquiry into questions, problems and issues that have relevance beyond the classroom, beyond the learners' immediate context, that are the same as questions that scientists, historians and educators pursue in the discipline, takes time. Ac-

cessing multiple perspectives and external expertise, analyzing and synthesizing historical data, gathering empirical data, interpreting first and second hand accounts, creating a
multimedia representation of one's new knowledge, takes sustained effort, social interaction and connection, access to rich and reliable and current information and knowledge,
and responsive and knowledgeable teachers and peers ("Perspiration versus Inspiration,"
2008, para. 2-3).

Inquiry is central, therefore, to 21st century learning and teaching, and to cultivate habits of mind consistent with such inquiry necessitates an understanding that:

> Inquiry is an approach to learning that involves a process of exploring the natural or ma-
> terial world, and that leads to asking questions, making discoveries, and rigorously test-
> ing those discoveries in the search for new understanding. Inquiry...should mirror as
> closely as possible the enterprise of doing real science. The inquiry process is driven by
> one's own curiosity, wonder, interest, or passion to understand an observation or solve a
> problem. The process begins when the learner notices something that intrigues, surprises,
> or stimulates a question--something that is new, or something that may not make sense in
> relationship to the learner's previous experience or current understanding. The next step is
> to take action--through continued observing, raising questions, making predictions, test-
> ing hypotheses, and creating theories and conceptual models. The learner must find his or
> her own pathway through this process. It is rarely a linear progression, but rather more of
> a back-and-forth, or cyclical, series of events. As the process unfolds, more observations
> and questions emerge, giving occasion for deeper interaction with the phenomena--and
> greater potential for further development of understanding. Along the way, the inquirer
> collects and records data, makes representations of results and explanations, and draws
> upon other resources such as books, videos, and the expertise or insights of others. Mak-
> ing meaning from the experience requires reflection, conversations, comparisons of find-
> ings with others, interpretation of data and observations, and the application of new con-
> ceptions to other contexts. All of this serves to help the learner construct a new mental
> framework of the world (Exploratorium Institute for Inquiry, n.d., para. 3-9).

The literature is replete with calls to cultivate habits of mind that are congruent with
reflective intelligence (that is, with mindfulness); whether in science education (Leager,
2005), in technology ("Perspiration versus Inspiration," 2008), in education in general
(Costa & Kallick, 2008), or in medicine (Epstein, 2003). In fact, while Costa and Kallick
(2008) maintain that habits of mind are critical to education in general, Epstein (2003)
contends that habits of mind are fundamental to effective medical practice, and even pro-
pose eight methods by and through which mindfulness (reflective intelligence) might be
cultivated: (a) Priming-setting the expectation of self-observation, (b) Availability – creating physical and mental space for exchange, (c) Reflective questions to open up possibilities and invite curiosity, (d) Active engagement-direct observation and exchange, (e)
Modeling while 'thinking out loud' to make mental processes more transparent, (f) Prac-

ticing attentiveness, curiosity, and presence, (g) Praxis-consolidation of learning by experience, and (h) Assessment and confirmation.

CHAPTER FOUR

ENHANCING REFLECTIVE INTELLIGENCE IN A GRADUATE SOCIAL FOUNDATIONS OF EDUCATION COURSE

> What if education were less about acquiring skills and knowledge and more about culti-
> vating the dispositions and habits of mind that students will need for a lifetime of learn-
> ing, problem solving, and decision making? What if education were less concerned with
> the end-of-year exam and more concerned with who students become as a result of their
> schooling? What if we viewed smartness as a goal that students can work toward rather
> than as something they either or don't? Re-envisioning education in this way implies that
> we will need to rethink many of our well-accepted methods of instruction. We will need
> to look beyond schools as training grounds for the memory and focus more on schooling
> as an enculturative process that cultivates dispositions of thinking [mindful educators]
> (Ritchhart, 2002, p. xxii).

Now it is time to use the ideas in Chapters 1, 2 and 3 to frame the kind of educative experience that facilitates dispositions arising as habits of mind for reflective intelligence.
Consequently, this chapter will describe efforts to enhance the habits of reflective intelligence in a graduate social foundations of education course in the College of Education at
Florida International University.

From Unit to Course

The College of Education (the Unit) in which this course is offered is guided by a conceptual framework that has as its vision "to facilitate diverse learning environments
where knowledge becomes the means to foster goal attainment for all those involved in
the learning process. This process will necessarily involve the highest ethical standards,
while emphasizing inquiry as the means-ends connection to enhancing reflective intelligence in a changing social, political, cultural and technological world" ("The Conceptual
Framework," n.d., p. 4). Such a vision reinforces the notion by Misco and Shiveley

(2007) that "When programs employ [inquiry] deliberation throughout the curriculum, the result is a unit-wide attempt to foster dispositions" (para. 17). The Unit's desired future is framed, therefore, by an explicit philosophy, the center from which the Unit approaches the preparation of its candidates, that enables the achieving of "a wisdom" which influences the conduct of life in the unit. The faculty in the Unit, therefore, seeks to create the kind of teaching and learning environments that elicit the mental and moral sensibilities consistent with reflective intelligence (The Conceptual Framework," n.d., p. 6). Consequently, teaching and learning, in the Unit, is seen through the lens of self-renewal "meant to help both candidates and faculty develop relevant intellectual and social dispositions that reinforce their being 'mindful' and thoughtful in their professional practice" (The Conceptual Framework," n.d., p. 6). In the Unit, habits of pedagogical mindfulness and thoughtfulness (reflective capacity):

> create a form of interconnectedness by which the unit's candidates have a disposition toward enhancing the growth of all learners through the application of their thinking to things already known (content, process skills) for the purpose of improving social conditions. This requires that teachers and other school personnel demonstrate commitments to patterns of intellectual activity that guide their cognitive and social behavior in educational settings with students, colleagues, families, and communities, thus enhancing their conduct in the world of practice – **mindful educators** ("The Conceptual Framework," n.d., pp. 10-11).

In the Unit, the habits of mind that make professional conduct more intelligent include candidates:

- Adopting a critical eye toward ideas and actions (Being Analytical).
- Withholding judgment until understanding is achieved by being thoughtful in [their] actions (Managing Impulsivity).
- Working to see things through by employing systematic methods [in] analyzing problems (Persisting).
- Thinking about [their] own thinking (Reflective Thoughtfulness).
- Thinking and communicating with clarity and precision (Communicating accurately).
- Showing curiosity and passion about learning through inquiry (Being Inquisitive).
- Showing a sense of being comfortable in situations where the outcomes are not immediately known by acting on the basis of [their] initiative and not from needing a script (Taking Responsible Risks).
- Recognizing the wholeness and distinctiveness of other people's ways of experiencing and making meaning by being open-minded (Being Open-minded).
- Taking time to check over work because of [their] being more interested in excellent work than in expediency (Striving for Accuracy).

- Abstracting meaning from one experience and carrying it forward and applying it to a new situation by calling on [their] store of past knowledge as a source of data to solve new challenges (Applying Past Knowledge to New Situations).
- Showing sensitivity to the needs of others and to being a cooperative team member (Thinking Interdependently), and,
- Showing a sense of care for others and an interest in listening well to others (Empathic Understanding) (Costa & Kallick, 2004 as cited in "The Conceptual Framework," n.d., p. 11).

The graduate course is built on the premise that a course in a Unit should facilitate candidates' learning what is valued in the Unit's Conceptual Framework. This idea is reinforced by Maki (2002) who states that an "Institution has to assure itself that it has translated its [vision] mission and purposes [philosophy] into its programs and services to more greatly assure that [candidates] have opportunities to learn and develop what an institution values....Without ample opportunity to reflect on and practice desired outcomes, [candidates] will not likely transfer, build upon, or deepen the learning and development an institution or program values" (p. 10). Furthermore, candidate learning proficiencies in the course should link to the learning outcomes in the Unit's Conceptual Framework. This link may be seen below.

Unit Learning Outcomes	Course Learning Proficiencies
Steward of the Discipline Know their content and engage in cross-disciplinary activities to ensure breadth and depth of knowledge. [SD 1 SD 3]	Understand and can apply knowledge from the humanities and social sciences to interpreting the meanings of education and schooling in diverse cultural contexts.
Reflective Inquirer Reflect on practice and change approaches based on own insights. [RI 1] Reflect on practice with the goal of continuous improvement. [RI 2] Think critically about issues through a form of inquiry that investigates dilemmas and problems and seek resolutions that benefit all involved. [RI3]	Understand and can apply critical perspectives on education and schooling by thinking critically about educational issues through a form of inquiry that investigates dilemmas and problems and seeks resolutions that benefit all involved.
Mindful Educator Being analytical; managing impulsivity; persisting; thinking about own thinking; communicating accurately; being inquisitive; taking responsible risks; being open-minded; striving for accuracy; applying past knowledge to new situations; thinking interdependently; showing a sense of care for others.	Be disposed to the intellectual and emotional habits of mind of: *being analytical; persisting; thinking about own thinking; managing impulsivity; being open-minded; striving for accuracy; communicating accurately; applying past knowledge to new situations; being inquisitive (taking responsible risks (primary.)* *thinking interdependently; showing a sense of care for others* (secondary).

Linking the course learning proficiencies to the Unit's learning outcomes is done also with the understanding that there has been a paradigm shift in education from focusing simply on teaching to focusing on candidate/student learning (Miller, 2006). The kind of professional educator the Unit is trying to produce is "a person who experiences continued capacity for growth, and who thus engages in intelligent action, that is, demonstrate wisdom in practice" ("The Conceptual Framework," n.d., p. 9). For instruction in the course to be consistent with the underlying philosophical and psychological beliefs in the Unit's Conceptual Framework, it must help candidates discover the connections between and among ideas, and it must facilitate fruitful learning experiences for candidates by helping them move beyond a transmission model of just absorbing information. Some of the pedagogical means by and through which the foregoing might be manifested include:

> Problem solving and decision making activities that incorporate technology;
> Cross-disciplinary and interdisciplinary learning;
> Cooperative learning;
> Activity-oriented and product-based pursuits;
> Faculty modeling expected moral behaviors;
> Providing encouragement and feedback;
> Helping candidates to construct, that is make meaningful the information they learned;
> Using varied teaching strategies;
> Faculty and candidates working as co-learners in their educational growth;
> Using assessments, both traditional and alternative/authentic ("The Conceptual Framework," n.d., p. 9).

Learning in the course is framed, therefore, as seen below:

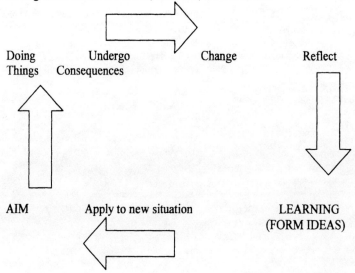

| Doing Things | Undergo Consequences | Change | Reflect |

| AIM | Apply to new situation | | LEARNING (FORM IDEAS) |

Learning in the graduate course is intended to enhance candidates' professional judgment. As such, to get learners to think like a professional is, according to Lee Shulman (2005) "a synthesis of three apprenticeships – a cognitive apprenticeship wherein one learns to think like a professional, a practical apprenticeship where one learns to perform like a professional, and a moral apprenticeship where one learns to think and act in a responsible and ethical manner that integrates across all three domains" (p. 3). Learning in the course is premised, therefore, on the following constructs: (a) that knowledge and skills must be acquired and used in order to enhance mindfulness and thoughtfulness, (b) that cognitive connections made through the acquisition of information and technical skill influences the formation of social dispositions/habits of mind, and (c) that working toward getting candidates to demonstrate dispositions/habits of mind through wisdom in practice is a moral endeavor not a technical matter.

Backward Course Design

L. Dee Fink (2003) cautions that if teachers want to create courses in which candidates have "significant learning experiences" then they must design that quality into their courses. One means by which to do so is "the backward course design" as advocated by Wiggins and McTighe (1998). In this process, one starts at the end of the learning process and works back toward the beginning. In many instances, professors in higher education institutions design courses by first looking for a textbook that contains course content information, and then second, by using the textbook chapters to outline class sessions for the semester. Such a process eschews significant learning experiences. As Wiggins and McTighe (1998) point out, the textbook simply contains the answers to the content. These authors argue that course designers should instead use the textbooks, and content area standards to seek the critical answer(s) to the content. In other words, look for the question(s) in the content to guide the learning experience.

So, my start in designing this graduate course begins with the assumption that the study of philosophy, history, and other basic disciplines of the humanities will help professional educators to develop interpretive, normative and critical perspectives on education. These perspectives, according to the Council for Social Foundations of Education (http://www.uic.edu/educ/csfe/index.htm), the society responsible for disseminating standards for foundations of education, are vital to any social foundations of education experience.

> The interpretive perspective-will assist learners in examining and explaining education within differing contexts; the normative perspective-will assist learners in examining and explaining education in light of value orientations; and the critical perspective-will assist learners in examining and explaining education in light of its origins, major influences, and consequences (Council for Social Foundations of Education, 1996, para, 12-14).

Professor Norm Bauer notes that "Interpretive, normative and critical thought are in reality intellectual skills and processes which we employ to explain, to make sense of, to comprehend the significance of our cognitive perspectives or structures" (Bauer, 1992, p. 6). On the other hand, a perusal of the literature with regard to foundations of education content suggests that education is seen in the light of asking important questions and finding fundamental answers to those questions (Butin, 2005; Osguthorpe, 2007; Tozer, Henry & Gallegos, forthcoming 2010). As a result, the essential question to guide learning in this graduate course is "Should schooling practices and policies be justified from ideological, philosophical, sociological, and historical perspectives?" It is assumed that to find answers to the essential question would require that teaching professionals acquire information and skills and use that information and those skills to act (inquire) thoughtfully and mindfully and thus enhance their professional judgment. Furthermore, to start with an essential question is the catalyst for inquiry.

So, the big question the course helps candidates address is "should schooling practices and policies be justified from ideological, philosophical, sociological, and historical perspectives?" The Backward Course Design next asks "What form of evidence might best demonstrate candidates' command of the essential question? This evidence becomes "the artifact" or the evidence of candidate learning; and, in this course, that artifact or evidence of learning is an argumentative, problem-inquiry paper.

The next step in The Backward Course Design is to articulate the essential elements in the task of creating and producing the artifact. The tenets of deliberative inquiry require that candidates (1) define a problem (they perceive in their field of study) that has moral, philosophical and universal implications (2) provide a literature review of the problem (3) analyze and argue their position on the problem through ideological, philosophical, sociological and historical lenses (4) provide reflections on the value of judgments to solve problem and (5) share a relevant bibliography of resources. The artifact will be shared as a written analytical paper, and should enable candidates to share their beliefs and arguments about the problem in their field through historical lenses, by offering ideological and philosophical justification, and by making relevant sociological connections. The task assumes that by pursuing social ends (the improvement of educational conditions), using content knowledge and thinking skills, certain intellectual, emotional, and social dispositions will be formed (moral sensibilities/dispositions or habits of mind that make professional action more intelligent and thus more ethical): questioning and posing problem, thinking flexibly, managing impulsivity, persisting, thinking about own thinking, striving for accuracy, thinking and communicating with clarity and precision, applying past knowledge to new situations, responding with wonderment and awe, taking responsible risks, thinking interdependently, demonstrating understanding and empathy.

Judging how well candidates perform on the task is the next critical step in the Backward Course Design. As a result, one must take the elements of the learning task, and delineate levels of performance on the task (e.g., outstanding, acceptable, unacceptable). In addition, it must be remembered that the creation and production of the artifact is also intended as means by and through which candidates show that the Unit is achieving its learning outcomes, in particular, enhancing and cultivating candidates' habits of mind.

Elements of the Task
Construct a moral/philosophical problem and lay out an introduction to that problem.
Use research information effectively to write a literature review on the problem question.
Understand and apply rules of reasoning to laying our arguments.
Present ideological/philosophical, sociological and historical arguments to support position on the problem.
Provide reflections on the value of judgments to solve the problem.
Outline references that meet APA Reference Style requirements.
Demonstrate good writing skills in argumentative/analytical paper.

Rubric

Elements of Task	Related COE Outcomes	Related Habits of Mind	Outstanding (3)	Acceptable (2)	Unacceptable (1)
Construct a moral/philosophical problem and lay out an introduction to that problem	Reflective Inquirer 1	Being analytical Think about own thinking	Shows outstanding evidence of a critical eye toward ideas, i.e., being analytical, thoughtful and reflective, and investigative, in clearly defining and introducing a moral, philosophical problem	Shows good evidence of a critical eye toward ideas, i.e., being analytical, thoughtful and reflective, and investigative, and investigative, in clearly defining and introducing a moral, philosophical problem	Shows little evidence of a critical eye toward ideas, i.e., being analytical, thoughtful and reflective, and investigative, in clearly defining and introducing a moral, philosophical problem

Elements of Task	Related COE Outcomes	Related Habits of Mind	Outstanding (3)	Acceptable (2)	Unacceptable (1)
Use research information effectively to write a literature review	Reflective Inquirer 3	Persisting – being focused and systematic Striving for accuracy Being inquisitive	Shows outstanding evidence of systematically working, by extending maximum effort, to broaden the knowledge base for the problem, i.e., write a comprehensive literature review; goes after material on own initiative.	Shows good evidence of systematically working, by extending maximum effort, to broaden the knowledge base for the problem, i.e., write a comprehensive literature review; goes after material with some direction.	Shows limited evidence of systematically working, by extending maximum effort, to broaden the knowledge base for the problem, i.e., write a comprehensive literature review; goes after material in a limited manner.

Elements of Task	Related COE Outcomes	Related Habits of Mind	Outstanding (3)	Acceptable (2)	Unacceptable (1)
Understand and apply rules of reasoning to laying out arguments	Reflective Inquirer 3	Thinking about own thinking	shows outstanding evidence of thinking about own thinking through the use of reasoning skills to structure arguments	shows good evidence of thinking about own thinking through the use of reasoning skills to structure arguments	shows limited evidence of thinking about own thinking through the use of reasoning skills to structure arguments

Elements of Task	Related COE Outcomes	Related Habits of Mind	Outstanding (3)	Acceptable (2)	Unacceptable (1)
Use ideas from readings as support to justify ideological/philosophical, sociological, and historical arguments vis-à-vis the problem question.	Steward of the Discipline 1 and 3	Managing impulsivity Thinking flexibly – being open minded	Shows outstanding evidence of deliberateness and open mindedness in being thoughtful in the use of ideas to justify a position on a problem	Shows good evidence of deliberateness and open mindedness in being thoughtful in the use of ideas to justify a position on a problem	Shows limited evidence of deliberateness and open mindedness in being thoughtful in the use of ideas to justify a position on a problem

Elements of Task	Related COE Outcomes	Related Habits of Mind	Outstanding (3)	Acceptable (2)	Unacceptable (1)
Provide reflections on how the value judgments in arguments will help to solve the educational problem	Reflective Inquirer 1 and 2	Apply past knowledge to new situation(s) Thinking about own thinking	Shows outstanding evidence of using knowledge acquired in arguments to ground recommendations for change in schooling realities (reflective thoughtfulness)	Shows good evidence of using knowledge acquired in arguments to ground recommendations for change in schooling realities (reflective thoughtfulness)	Shows limited evidence of using knowledge acquired in arguments to ground recommendations for change in schooling realities (reflective thoughtfulness)

Elements of Task	Related COE Outcomes	Related Habits of Mind	Outstanding (3)	Acceptable (2)	Unacceptable (1)
References that meet APA Reference Style requirements	Reflective Inquirer 3	Striving for accuracy	Shows outstanding evidence of striving for accuracy by providing a comprehensive bibliography of relevant sources and exactness in APA citations in the narrative and reference section .	Shows good evidence of striving for accuracy by providing a comprehensive bibliography of relevant sources and exactness in APA citations in the narrative and reference section.	Shows limited evidence of striving for accuracy by providing a comprehensive bibliography of relevant sources and exactness in APA citations in the narrative and reference section

Elements of Task	Related COE Outcomes	Related Habits of Mind	Outstanding (3)	Acceptable (2)	Unacceptable (1)
Writing skills in argumentative paper	Reflective Inquirer 3	Thinking and communicating with clarity and precision	Shows outstanding evidence of thinking and communicating with clarity and precision by exhibiting command of the language and correct use of grammar and syntax	Shows good evidence of thinking and communicating with clarity and precision by exhibiting command of the language and correct use of grammar and syntax.	Shows limited evidence of thinking and communicating with clarity and precision by exhibiting command of the language and correct use of grammar and syntax

College of Education Outcomes: **Steward of the Discipline:** Know their content (SD 1) and engage in cross-disciplinary activities to ensure breadth and depth of knowledge (SD 3). **Reflective Inquirer:** Reflect on practice and change approaches based on own insights (RI 1), Reflect on practice with the goal of continuous improvement (RI 2), and

Think critically about issues through a form of inquiry that investigates dilemmas and problems and seek resolutions that benefit all involved (RI 3). **Mindful Educator:** Being analytical; managing impulsivity; persisting; thinking about own thinking; communicating accurately; being inquisitive; taking responsible risks; being open-minded; striving for accuracy; applying past knowledge to new situations; thinking interdependently; showing a sense of care for others.

The Backward Course Design concludes with the experiences in the course that will enhance candidate learning. The class sessions are therefore organized to facilitate the learning of content, process skills and habits of mind germane to each element of the course artifact, that is, the argumentative, problem-inquiry paper. The process is captured below:

Learning at each stage  Applying Learning at each
Doing and undergoing stage of paper development

Learning Objective(s)   **Use what is acquired to inquire**
Acquire knowledge and skills

REFLECTION
Calling forth habits of mind
Each class member reflects on
whether he/she demonstrated
the habits of mind called forth
at the respective stage and
writes his/her reflection in the
Habits of Mind Inventory

Meeting standards
Each group reflects on
whether the learning at the
respective stage meets
standards (College, State,
Professional) and writes the
group reflection in the
Meeting Standards Template

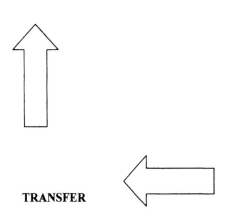

TRANSFER

Learning in the course is framed, therefore, by the idea that enhancing the growth of teacher education candidates through the application of their thinking to things already known (content and process skills) for the purpose of improving social conditions is to help them acquire dispositions, both intellectual and social, in other words, acquire the habits that render their conduct intelligent:

Only that which has been organized into our *dispositions* so as to enable us to adapt the environment to our needs and to adapt our aims and desires to the situation in which we live is really knowledge. Knowledge is not just some thing which we are conscious of, but consists of the *dispositions* we consciously use in understanding what now happens. Knowledge as an act is bringing some of our dispositions to consciousness with a view to straightening out a perplexity, by conceiving the connection between ourselves and the world in which we live (Dewey, 1916/1944, p. 344).

On the other hand, the learning experiences are intended to help candidates get into the habit of linking and constructing meaning from their experiences in the course. According to Costa and Kallick (2008) "Such work requires reflection" (221).

Reflecting on work enhances its meaning. Reflecting on experiences encourages insight and complex learning. We foster our own growth when we control our learning, so some reflection is best done alone. Reflection is also enhanced, however, when we ponder our learning with others. Reflection involves linking a current experience to previous learning a process called *scaffolding*. Reflection also involves drawing forth cognitive and emotional information from several sources: visual, auditory, kinesthetic, and tactile. To reflect, we must act upon and process the information, synthesizing and evaluating the data. In the end, reflecting also means applying what we've learned to contexts beyond the original situation in which we learned something (Costa and Kallick, 2008, pp. 221-222).

Learning Experiences Process

The learning experiences in the course are laid out in modules that are guided by a specific learning objective. The learning experiences therefore delineate the content and process skills to be acquired, the habits of mind to enhance intelligent action, and the assessments for learning that contribute to candidates' continued capacity to grow. The learning objectives are delineated below:

Learning Objective 1- Given a working prompt by the instructor, candidates working in learning communities will, through consensus, formulate a moral, philosophical problem question in the field of education and using a template provided by the instructor prepare a brief written introduction to the problem question by contrasting the pros and cons in the problem and by laying out the paper's components (synthesis).

Knowledge-concepts, facts, principles to comprehend-Ethical vision of education (ideas and their significance; meaning and necessity of philosophy of education. Kinds of questions.

Procedures, processes to master and demonstrate-Brainstorming – thinking outside the box. Group process skills – managerial (mechanisms by which community acts as a unit and not as a loose rabble) and interpersonal (basic manners).

Dispositions (habits of mind) to make judgment more intelligent-[1] Being investigative and adopting a critical eye toward ideas and actions; [3] Being thoughtful and reflective; [9] Bringing a freshness of mind to bear on issues, problems, concerns; [10] Acting on

the basis of own heart and will rather than in ways that are scripted by forces not of own making; [11] Demonstrating teamwork
Assessment-how performance will be monitored and assessed- Assessment of understanding through oral questioning. Assessment of skills through observations and checklists. Assessment of habits of mind through HoM Inventory and self-assessment.

Learning Objective II- After a presentation by the instructor on literature review, and participating in an information inquiry and research strategies session with a Reference Librarian, candidates in their learning communities will use research information effectively to write a literature review of key concepts in the problem question (application).

Knowledge-concepts, facts, principles to comprehend-Search strategy techniques–know about keywords, synonyms, Boolean, truncation, adjacency, subject headings/descriptors; Know about relevant databases; Know about search tools; Know about criteria to evaluate quality of web resources; Know if library owns something; Know basic APA citation requirements.

Procedures, processes to master and demonstrate-Be able to conduct a literature review using electronic technologies. Be able to write a literature review. Demonstrate group process skills - managerial (mechanisms by which community acts as a unit and not as a loose rabble) and interpersonal (basic manners). Brainstorming – thinking outside the box. Group process skills – managerial (mechanisms by which community acts as a unit and not as a loose rabble) and interpersonal (basic manners).

Dispositions (habits of mind) to make judgment more intelligent-[4] Being focused and systematic; [6] Striving for accuracy (exactness and correctness); *[7] Thinking and communicating with clarity and precision; [11] Demonstrating teamwork* [1] Being investigative and adopting a critical eye toward ideas and actions; [3] Being thoughtful and reflective; *[9] Bringing a freshness of mind to bear on issues, problems, concerns; [10] Acting on the basis of own heart and will rather than in ways that are scripted by forces not of own making; [11]Demonstrating teamwork.*

Assessment-how performance will be monitored and assessed-Assessment of understanding through Pre- Post- Quiz. Assessment of skills through observations and checklists. Assessment of habits of mind through HoM Inventory and self-assessment.

Learning Objective III- After presentations by the instructor, candidates in learning communities will sketch/structure argument(s) for the community's argumentative paper (application).

Knowledge-concepts, facts, principles to comprehend-Know the kinds of arguments
Know the forms of arguments.

Procedures, processes to master and demonstrate-Be able to check the validity of an argument. Be able to justify an argument. Demonstrate group process skills - managerial (mechanisms by which community acts as a unit and not as a loose rabble) and interpersonal (basic manners).

Dispositions (habits of mind) to make judgment more intelligent-[5] Thinking about own thinking; *[3] Being thoughtful and reflective; [11] Demonstrating teamwork.*
Assessment-how performance will be monitored and assessed-Assessment of understanding through constructed response questions. Assessment of skills through constructed response questions and checklists. Assessment of habits of mind through HoM Inventory and self-assessment.

Learning Objective IV-After participating in a series of analytical focus discussions on ideological and philosophical readings assigned by the instructor, candidates in learning communities will use ideas from the readings as support to justify the community's ideological/philosophical argument vis-à-vis the problem question (application).

Knowledge-concepts, facts, principles to comprehend- Understand various ideologies and philosophic schools of thought: ideologies of conservatism, liberalism, and schools of thought: idealism (Plato), and pragmatism, progressivism (Dewey).
Procedures, processes to master and demonstrate- Group process skills - managerial (mechanisms by which community acts as a unit and not as a loose rabble) and interpersonal (basic manners)
Dispositions (habits of mind) to make judgment more intelligent-*[1] Adopting a critical eye toward ideas and actions;* [2] Seeing different perspectives; [3] Being thoughtful and reflective; *5] Thinking about own thinking; [8] Applying past knowledge to new situations; [11] Being cooperative; [12] Being attuned and respectful*
Assessment-how performance will be monitored and assessed- Assessment of facts, concepts through multiple-choice questions. Assessment of skills through observations and checklists. Assessment of habits of mind through HoM Inventory and self-assessment.

Learning Objective IV-After participating in a series of analytical focus discussions on ideological and philosophical readings assigned by the instructor, candidates in learning communities will use ideas from the readings as support to justify the community's sociological argument vis-à-vis the problem question (application).

Knowledge-concepts, facts, principles to comprehend-Understand various social theories: functionalist theory, conflict theory, interactionist theory, interpretivist theory and sociological content: conflict theory, education/conflict theory, education/functionalist theory, family/functionalism, family/conflict theory, symbolic interactionism).
Procedures, processes to master and demonstrate- Group process skills - managerial (mechanisms by which community acts as a unit and not as a loose rabble) and interpersonal (basic manners)
Dispositions (habits of mind) to make judgment more intelligent-*[1] Adopting a critical eye toward ideas and actions;* [2] Seeing different perspectives; [3] Being thoughtful and reflective; *5] Thinking about own thinking; [8] Applying past knowledge to new situations; [11] Being cooperative; [12] Being attuned and respectful*
 Assessment-how performance will be monitored and assessed- Assessment of facts, concepts through multiple-choice questions. Assessment of skills through
observations and checklists. Assessment of habits of mind through HoM Inventory and self-assessment.

Learning Objective IV-After participating in a series of analytical focus discussions on ideological and philosophical readings assigned by the instructor, candidates in learning communities will use ideas from the readings as support to justify the community's historical argument vis-à-vis the problem question (application).

Knowledge-concepts, facts, principles to comprehend-Understand various historical events in American education (historical content: liberty and literacy; school as a public institution; teaching in a public institution: the professionalization movement; social diversity and differentiated schooling; and school reform).

Procedures, processes to master and demonstrate- Group process skills - managerial (mechanisms by which community acts as a unit and not as a loose rabble) and interpersonal (basic manners)

Dispositions (habits of mind) to make judgment more intelligent-*[1] Adopting a critical eye toward ideas and actions;* [2] Seeing different perspectives; [3] Being thoughtful and reflective; *5] Thinking about own thinking; [8] Applying past knowledge to new situations; [11] Being cooperative; [12] Being attuned and respectful*

Assessment-how performance will be monitored and assessed- Assessment of facts, concepts through multiple-choice questions. Assessment of skills through observations and checklists. Assessment of habits of mind through HoM Inventory and self-assessment.

Learning Objective V- After being given a working prompt by the instructor, candidates in learning communities will judge how the value judgments in the argument(s) will help to solve the problem in schools today.
(evaluate)

Knowledge-concepts, facts, principles to comprehend- Understand that appraisal of value judgments results in new valuing (tool for discovering how to live a better life

Procedures, processes to master and demonstrate-. Compare and contrast current schooling realities with value judgments in arguments. Use empirical findings to assess relevance of value judgments. Group process skills - managerial (mechanisms by which community acts as a unit and not as a loose rabble) and interpersonal (basic manners)

Dispositions (habits of mind) to make judgment more intelligent-[5] Thinking about own thinking; [8] Applying past knowledge to new situations

Assessment-how performance will be monitored and assessed- Assessment of understanding through oral questioning. Assessment of skills through observations and checklists. Assessment of habits of mind through HoM Inventory and self-assessment.

The syllabus for the course (The Map for the educational journey) is laid out to facilitate the foregoing "backward course design."

Syllabus Components
Course Demographics
Name and Number of Course
Department
Web site for course
Credits

Name of Instructor
E-mail address
Office hours
Office location
Telephone/fax number(s)
Resources for course (texts, etc.)
Grading criteria
Purpose of Course
Link to the Unit's Conceptual Framework's Outcomes
Course Learning Outcomes
Unit of Study Design
   Essential Question to Guide Learning
   Performance Task/Artifact
   Requisite knowledge, skills and habits of mind (needed to complete
   task/artifact)
   Scoring Rubric for Artifact
   Learning Experiences/Learning Objectives
   Learning Objectives Aligned with Standards (College, State and Prof-
   essional)
   Learning Schedule/Class Sessions
Other Assessments
   Group performance
   Class participation
Other Resources

From Course Design to Nurturing Habits of Mind

A theory of learning is critical to framing learning experiences in the course. As a result, Kolb's learning cycle ("Kolb Learning Cycle," n.d.) helps to shape the learning experiences and practices during each Learning Objective (see model below). This process of "reflection on action" enables learners to stop and examine why they acted as they did, and, as a result, gain insight from the learning experience. In other words, candidates get to formulate relationships and continuities among the elements of the experience in each Learning Objective and to bring to awareness the habits of mind by and through which they value the personal and intellectual growth of others. This is the condition of active learning characterized by continuity and growth.

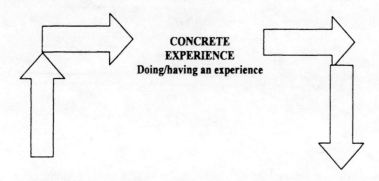

CONCRETE
EXPERIENCE
Doing/having an experience

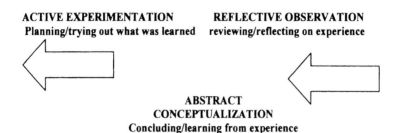

ACTIVE EXPERIMENTATION   **REFLECTIVE OBSERVATION**
Planning/trying out what was learned   reviewing/reflecting on experience

ABSTRACT
CONCEPTUALIZATION
Concluding/learning from experience

Adapted   from   Kolb   Learning   Cycle   Tutorial-Static   Version
(http://www.ldu.leeds.ac.uk/ldu/sddu_multimedia/kolb/static_version.php

> We never educate directly, but indirectly by means of the environment. Whether we per-
> mit chance environments to do the work, or whether we design environments for the pur-
> pose makes a great difference. And any environment is a chance environment so far as its
> educative influence is concerned unless it has been deliberately regulated with reference
> to its educative effect. An intelligent home differs from an unintelligent one chiefly in
> that the habits of life and intercourse which prevail are chosen, or at least colored, by the
> thought of their bearing upon the development of children (Dewey, 1916/1944, p. 19).

John Dewey's words above, provides critical insight with regard to teaching and learning and the importance of nurturing an educative environment. It should be noted that
Dewey insisted that not all experiences are educative, since mere activity does not constitute an educative experience. Educators can nurture educative experiences by helping
students to discover the connections between and among things, and ideas, and not by
just having students ingest information (Hansen, 2002). Helping students to learn from
experience obliges them to extend and deepen their interest in learning from all contacts
in the world, and to cultivate moral traits and attitudes toward thinking and acting in the
world (Hansen, 2002). An educative environment is therefore a form of associated life
that fuels the growth of both the individual and the group (Hansen, 2002).

Dewey helps us see that the environment supports or hinders the cultivation of habits
of mind, and, therefore, "If teachers cultivate and support conditions that engage students
in an activity…learning will more likely be the outcome" (Hansen, 2002, p. 277). So,
"give the pupils something to do, not something to learn; and the doing is of such a nature
as to demand thinking or the intentional noting of connections; learning naturally results"
(Dewey, 1916/1944, p. 154).

Educative experiences engender candidates to acquire meaning by reflecting on their
actions, and since good judgment is needed for reflection, then judgment formed from an
educative experience is shaped by and through reflective habits [of mind]. Hansen (2002)
says that the following conditions must exist in order to bring an educative environment
into being: (a) the objects in the experience must draw [candidates] into acting instead of

being lectured to and about, (b) the activities and exchanges must call out the best thinking in candidates and must fuel the emergence of moral dispositions, (c) [candidates]
must be able to pursue their own educational interests and adventures while interacting
with others in ways that deepen and widen social sympathies, (d) the activities must invite [candidates] to see the interrelatedness of knowledge, skills and dispositions, (e) such
negative forces as anti-intellectualism, intolerance, etc., must be eschewed, and (f) the
teacher must be knowledgeable and embody the essential habits of mind.

On the other hand, we are reminded by Ritchhart (2002) and Lakoff and Johnson
(1980) that attention to language, routines, and the use of metaphors are critical in nurturing dispositions in educative environments in that they all structure the actions we perform, that is, influence our conduct .

CHAPTER FIVE

ENHANCING REFLECTIVE INTELLIGENCE IN A GRADUATE SOCIAL FOUNDATIONS OF EDUCATION COURSE: THE SESSIONS

Introductory Course Session 1

The goal in the first introductory course session is to (1) get candidates to realize that they are going on an educational journey (use of metaphor) in which they will be learning from experience, and (2) bring to their awareness the things for the journey that they should (a) know about (the professor's philosophy of education and what the literature says about the goals for a social foundations of education course), (b) complete (such as an information sheet), (c) have (such as the map-the metaphor for the syllabus, the templates for the Argumentative Problem-Inquiry Paper, and the Habits of Mind Inventory), do (such as acquire an account with the commercial e-Folio system, Taskstream, the system to which they will upload their course artifacts), and examine (examples of papers completed by candidates in previous courses/journeys).

I begin the session by inviting candidates to share three things that to them make a journey rewarding, and three things that make a journey disappointing, and I then ask them to reflect on their responses to identify any common underlying insights. I also invite them to share three key positive things from the best educational experience they have had, and three key negative things from the worst educational experience. Again, I ask them to reflect on their responses to identify any common underlying insights. I use the underlying insights to examine their relevance for the present educational journey.

Next, I ask candidates to spell the following words, most, boast, and roast, at the end of which I pose the question: what do you put in a toaster? Some candidates will say toast, and a few will say bread. Without addressing the correctness or incorrectness of responses, I note that schooling is usually more concerned with "the right answer," but this educational journey is interested in what candidates learn. As a result, I am more interested in what was learned from the spelling activity. To help class members focus on learning, I ask them if a child sticks its finger in a flame and is burned has the child learned. I use their responses as the opportunity to help them realize that if a child sticks its finger in a flame, that learning occurs only when the child connects the physical pain and visible skin reaction from the action, and draws the insight that fire burns. So, as candidates reflect more on the spelling scenario they come to realize that to follow like sounding words can induce a non-thinking reaction, and thus they acquire meaning from the experience (that is, to learn from experience). I enable class members to capture the foregoing idea visually through the diagram below:

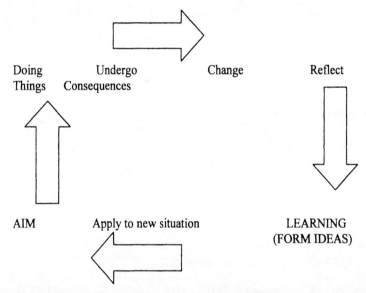

Doing   Undergo   Change   Reflect
Things   Consequences

AIM   Apply to new situation   LEARNING
                                            (FORM IDEAS)

   The foregoing activity enables me to direct class members' focus to the concept of reflection that is needed to formulate the relationships and continuities between and among the elements of an experience, and by extension, to consider the concept of "the mind," as being involved in meaning-making, as well as to the realization that their conduct is made more intelligent by being "reflective," that is, being mindful, and that consistent reflective action requires "habits of mind" that value the personal and intellectual growth of self and of others. They are then brought to the realization that the College of Education has as an outcome for them to be "mindful educators" who by nature must be "reflective inquirers" and "stewards of the discipline."
   Since candidates bring habits to the educational journey, I next highlight this by asking class members to share some ideas that come to their minds based on their previous experiences in taking courses. I provide the example of the idea of a student always having

to take a mid-term and final examination in the courses he/she has taken previously. I ask class members what habits they might have formed from their previous course taking experiences. I use the exam taking example to show that the habit of memorizing and approaching things in the same way may be formed from the experience of always engaging in mid-term and final examinations. That these habits that are formed and are used in new situations is then brought to the fore by showing that the candidate who has formed the habit of memorizing and approaching things the same way may ask automatically at the start of a new course about obtaining the textbook so that he/she may start preparing for the tests. I explain that if that candidate is in a course that does not use a textbook, per se, or utilize mid-term and final examinations, then that student's habit is blocked, and he/she may engage in behavior in which he/she complains that the new situation makes no sense, and engenders too much work.

> Activity runs the path of habit until it is blocked by an obstacle. In the face of blocked activity, impulse emerges and seeks an outlet in activity. In seeking the outlet, the old (habit) and the new (impulse) collide, producing a problem. Intellect mediates between habit and impulse (Reynolds, 1993, p. 30).

I help class members realize that the conditions that constitute habit are found not in the individual, but in the social order; hence changing individuals will not alter habits profoundly; social conditions must also change. To begin to assess candidates' awareness of their habits of mind, I share the following 12 habits of mind (questioning, being open-minded, being thoughtful, persisting, thinking about own thinking, striving for accuracy, communicating with clarity and precision, transferring knowledge to new situations, showing a curiosity and passion for learning, taking responsible risks, thinking interdependently, and listening well to others and caring for others), and I ask candidates to indicate, based on what he/she has heard, done and/or seen in the first introductory session on the educational journey, to identify the habits of mind that they think they might start to demonstrate, stop demonstrating or continue demonstrating on this educational journey.

To acquire knowledge of students at the start of any learning experience is a critical component in the learning process. Consequently, I ask candidates to do two things that I call pre-journey checks. First, I ask them to identify an educational practice or policy that they believe will improve some aspect of education for teachers, or students, or administrators, or counselors, and so on). I also require that they provide a brief justification for the practice or policy by using the prompt "This practice or policy ought to occur because...." and delineate the ideological, philosophical, social theory and/or historical ideas to support their position that the practice or policy ought to occur. Next, I show them the question, Should the College of Education at FIU admit only graduate students with a Graduate Record Exam (GRE) score above 1100? and a response to the question presented by a college student, and ask them to state (1) the structure of the student's argument, and (2) indicate whether the student's argument is valid or invalid:

> Test exams are not indicative of knowledge of testee. The College of Education (COE) wants knowledgeable, good students. Admission of only graduate students with GRE scores of 1100 and above does not guarantee admittance of knowledgeable students. Therefore, the COE should not limit admissions into programs to GRE scores.

The responses from the foregoing enable me to gain a feel for class participants' ability to justify educational policies or practices, and their knowledge of arguments.

At this point, I take the opportunity to guide class members to the WebCT/Blackboard online course system for the things needed for the journey: (a) things to know about-the professor's philosophy of education and what the literature says should be the goals for a social foundations of education course, (b) things to complete-an information sheet, (c) things to have-the syllabus (the map), the template for the argumentative paper, the template for the meeting standards reflections, the template for the habits of mind inventory, (d) things to do-acquire an account on the Taskstream electronic system, (e) things to examine-examples of completed argumentative papers.

It is at this point in the first introductory session that the words of Diana Kelly (n.d.) become poignant:

> In higher education we sometimes pause at the end of a lecture and ask, "Any questions?" or "Is everything clear?" Usually there are no responses, and as students leave we are satisfied that we did allow students the opportunity to ask questions. However, how do we really know what students are actually learning when they are in the process of learning something new for the first time? As lecturers we are not mind readers. We need to check in with our students to find out what they are learning and what they don't fully understand (para. 1).

So, to gain a sense of what candidates in EDF 6608 are learning in the first introductory session, I utilize an informal means (the minute paper) and ask them to provide a written response to the following questions: (1) Did this class experience give you any insights regarding the kind of educational journey you will experience, and (2) Did this class experience reaffirm or change any expectations you may have had about the course?

Introductory Course Session II

The second introductory session enables both professor and candidates to look back and reflect on what they learned from the first session with regard to: (a) their minute paper feedback, (b) their pre-journey abilities vis-à-vis knowledge of philosophy of education, social theory and history of education, and arguments, and (c) the habits of mind that class members think they might start demonstrating, stop demonstrating, or continue demonstrating on the educational journey.

Since I must be sure that class members are clear about the meaning of the habits of mind that will render their professional conduct more intelligent, I use the second introductory session to walk through each habit of mind and its related conduct indicators as seen below:

1. Habit of Mind: Adopt a critical eye toward ideas and actions
To adopt a questioning attitude (questioning and posing problems) versus not asking questions to fill in unknown gaps (unquestioning)
Ask questions to fill in the gap between what is known and what is not known; Pose questions about alternative positions or points of view; Probe into the causes of things or just accepted things as they are; Pose questions that required a yes or no answer or pose more complex questions.

2. Habit of Mind Being open-minded
To be open-minded *(thinking flexibly)* versus changing mind even in light of new data *(closed minded)*
Change mind based on new credible data; Approach things in the same way (the way to which he/she has become most accustomed; Perceive things from perspectives other than his/her own; Tolerate ambiguity up to a point.

3. Habit of Mind: Being thoughtful in actions
To withhold value judgment about an idea until understanding is achieved *(manage impulsivity)* versus blurt out the first answer that comes to mind *(acts without forethought)*
Act and then think or think before acting; Strive to clarify and understand what he/she heard and read, etc?; Jump to offer an opinion about something that he/she does not understand fully; Consider different possibilities before taking action; Accept the first idea that came to mind.

4. Habit of Mind: Work to see things through
To persevere on the task even though the resolution is not immediately apparent *(persisting)* VERSUS write down and/or say things just to be done with the task at hand quickly *(despairs easily)*
Stick to tasks until it is completed or give up easily; Set up a systematic system to guide his/her completing tasks; Give up easily when the answer to something is not immediately known; Stay on focus throughout the learning experience or is easily distracted.

5. Habit of Mind: Think about own thinking
To reflect on my experience(s) (thinking about own thinking) versus not take time to reflect on my experience(s) (unthoughtful)
Plan for, reflect on, and evaluate the quality of own thinking; Is increasingly aware of his/her actions on others; Develop and use mental maps or rehearse before he/she performs an action; Reflects on his/her actions (what he/she did); Wonders about why he/she is doing what he/she is doing; Explains his/her decision-making process on matters.

6. Habit of Mind: Take time to check over work

To find reworking task acceptable because of more interest in excellent work than in expediency (striving for accuracy) versus more anxious to complete task than to take time
to check for accuracy and precision (no pride in work)

*Work to produce excellent work; Check over what he/she produced; Works to perfect
his/her work; Holds to high standards any work he/she produces.*

7. Habit of Mind: Think and communicate with clarity and precision

To use clear language and thinking in both written and oral forms *(thinking and communicating with clarity and precision) versus* use fuzzy language and thinking in both written and oral forms *(vague and fuzzy thinking and writing)*

*Is clear in his/her writing and speaking; Uses fuzzy language and thinking; Uses precise
language and defines terms and ideas clearly; Uses good thinking skills and logic.*

8. Habit of Mind: Transfer learning to new situation

To begin new task by making connections to prior experience and knowledge (applying
past knowledge to new situations) versus begin new task as if it were being approached
for the first time and make no connection to prior experience (does not transfer knowledge)

*Learns from his/her experiences; Draws on past experience to solve present problems
(situations); Approaches each new task as though it were the first time; Recalls how
he/she may have solved something in the past that is similar to something on which he is
now working; Applies something he/she learned previously in a new situation.*

9. Habit of Mind: Show curiosity and passion about learning

To have fun figuring things out *(responding with wonderment and awe) versus* perceive
thinking as hard work and recoil from situations that demand too much of it *(no passion
about learning, inquiry and mastering work)*

*Is turned on about learning new things; Likes things that require hard thinking; Is curi-
ous about ordinary things; Is interested in inquiring into how and why things are; Wants
to master what he has to do.*

10. Habit of Mind: Act on the basis of own initiative

To be more interested in being challenged by the process of finding the answer than in
just knowing the answer is correct *(take responsible risks) versus* be more interested in
knowing the answer is correct than being challenged by the process of finding the answer
(fears failure)

*Goes beyond established limits; Is comfortable in situations whose outcomes are not im-
mediately clear; Accepts failure as part of his/her own growth; Accepts setbacks as challenging and growth producing; Knows when to take educated risks and when not to take
impulsive risks; Takes a chance in the moment or only after he has calculated all costs;
Only knows the correct answer or is challenged by the process of finding the answer.*

11.Habit of Mind: Be a cooperative team member

To contribute to group work by being able to work and learn from others in reciprocal
situations *(thinking interdependently) versus* not contribute to group work either by being
a "job hog" or by letting others do all the work *(prefers solitude)*

*Draws energy from others and seeks reciprocity; Prefers solitary work; Is sensitive to the
needs of others; Is a job hog; just wants to do things only with him/herself; Lets oth-*

ers do all the work for him/her; Is excited about having to justify and test his/her ideas on others; Is willing to accept feedback from a critical friend
12.Habit of Mind: Care for others and listen well to others
To devote mental energy to understanding others' thoughts and feelings *(listening with understanding and empathy)* versus not paying close attention to what is being said beneath the words *(hears but does not listen)*
Speaks when others are speaking or does he listen carefully when others are speaking; Paraphrases what he/she hears others say and accurately expresses what was said; Attends carefully to what others say beneath their words; Holds in abeyance his/her judgments and opinions so he/she can listen to another person's thoughts and ideas.

Once class members acquire a better understanding of each habit of mind, I then ask them to rate their expected conduct on the educational journey on each of the 12 habits of mind. The Self-Rating Scale is provided in Appendix A.

I then move to explain the set up of the educational journey as a backward course design. This enables class members to focus on (a) the essential question to guide learning on the educational journey, (b) the artifact that will be evidence of their answering the essential question, (c) the knowledge, skills, and habits of mind needed to produce a quality artifact, (d) the criteria by which the final artifact will be judged-the rubric, and (e) the necessary learning sessions.

I help candidates make more sense of the design of the learning process on the journey by noting that they will be doing and undergoing the consequences of their doing at each stage of the journey, and they will be asked to apply the learning from their acquired knowledge and skills to the development of their argumentative paper. To do so, however, will call forth certain habits of mind, and each class member will be asked to reflect on his/her actions with regard to whether he or she demonstrated the respective habits of mind, write his/her reflections in the Habits of Mind Inventory (an Inventory developed by the author)-see Appendix B. Since growth in reflective intelligence is not just an individual matter, but a social one as well, I ask class members to reflect, as a member of the small groups in the course, on their learning at each stage in the journey, and link that learning to the relevant candidate proficiencies in Institutional Standards (College of Education), State of Florida Standards (Florida Educator Accomplished Practices), and Professional Standards (National Board for Professional Teaching Standards). The Meeting Standards Template is provided in Appendix C.

I use the diagram below to help class members visual the foregoing.

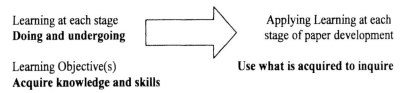

Learning at each stage
Doing and undergoing

Learning Objective(s)
Acquire knowledge and skills

Applying Learning at each
stage of paper development

Use what is acquired to inquire

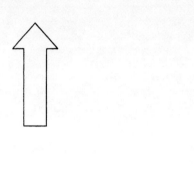

REFLECTION
Calling forth habits of mind
Each class member reflects on
whether he/she demonstrated
the habits of mind called forth
at the respective stage and
writes his/her reflection in the
Habits of Mind Inventory

Meeting standards
Each group reflects on
whether the learning at the
respective stage meets
standards (College, State,
Professional) and writes the
group reflection in the
Meeting Standards Template

TRANSFER

Since the literature suggests that reflection must be taught (Spalding and Wilson (2002), I provide an example of a reflection from a Habits of Mind Inventory and one from a Meeting Standards Template, and asks candidates to examine the reflections using the following set of reflective criteria to judge the reflective writing in the examples: (a) does the reflective writing move from superficial to in-depth reflections, (b) does the writing make specific references to learning events, (c) does it provide examples and elaborations, (d) does it make connections to other learning, and (e) does it discuss modifications based on insights from insights.

Example of Reflection from Habits of Mind Inventory
I have been asked to "reflect" on my learning by my professor. The unit of learning, or "learning objective 1" as referred to by my professor, or "step 1" by a class colleague, was about my working with other group members to identify a moral/philosophical problem question of which our group was very interested, and write an introduction section of an argumentative paper in which my group highlighted the pros and cons surrounding the problem and indicated the structure of our argumentative paper. Completing the above has been an eye opening experience for me. At the first class session of the semester, I was rearing to go, as I usually am in my courses. I would get a syllabus, it would tell me what textbook to buy, I would get a head start by reading chapter 1, since the teachers always started with lectures on chapter 1, and the head start would give me a leg up on the obligatory forthcoming quiz on the information in the chapter. Wow! Was my way of having done things shaken up in this experience. The professor said I did not need to read anything to start this learning experience. Was he kidding! You only learn from reading the information in the textbook. We started "Learning Objective 1" and the professor laid

out the goal for our learning, the knowledge, skills, and habits of mind that would be needed. It did not hit me, initially, that if I let myself be open to working on acquiring these things that in so doing I might make connections between the knowledge, skills I was acquiring and what that knowledge and skill was enabling me to now do that I was unable to do previously. But, as we worked on the content, I realized I did not know the difference between "moral" and "ethics." Under normal circumstances, I would have brushed off my not knowing, and simply scanned the textbook index for the answer. But, something moved me to ask the professor help me fill in the gap between what I knew and did not know, and suddenly I was gaining insights about the argumentative paper on which we were working; that we were learning about ideas, and not just receiving information; and since, one cannot give another ideas, then that was why the professor was laying out some things, but setting up the environment in such a way that if I and my colleagues focused on what we were doing, and undergoing in the Learning Objective, and connected that to what we were to do on the argumentative paper that my mind started to see things. For example, I suddenly started to see that what we were going to be writing about was about human conduct and about how life ought to be lived in schools and educational institutions. AND to explore such was MORAL! Bingo!!!!! Now, I was no longer interested in my group producing a problem question that we could just answer, "yes" or "no." Hey, when one group member said, "just let us tell the professor our topic for the paper will be how to group students, I asked her to explain what bothered her about group students that might give insight into how we ought to live." Did I just learn to be "mindful"?

Example of Reflection from Meeting Standards Template

What do the College of Education standards require? The standards require that a candidate be a:

Reflective Inquirer
Reflect on practice and change approaches based on own insights.
Reflect on practice with the goal of continuous improvement.
Think critically about issues through a form of inquiry that investigates dilemmas and problems and seek resolutions that benefit all involved.

Mindful Educator
Being analytical; managing impulsivity; persisting; thinking about own thinking; communicating accurately; being inquisitive; taking responsible risks; being open-minded; striving for accuracy; applying past knowledge to new situations; thinking interdependently; showing a sense of care for others.

What did WE come to know, be able to do or be disposed toward in LEARNING OBJECTIVE #1 that is representative of what the standard calls for?

Learning Objective #1: To formulate a moral, philosophical problem question, and prepare a brief written introduction to the problem question by contrasting the pros and cons in the problem and by laying out the paper's components.

Learning is doing and undergoing the consequences and reflecting on the change. Our professor asked us to divide money equally among some class members, and we did. He then asked us to divide the same amount of money fairly, and we hesitated. Why did we hesitate? Suddenly, as we reflected we realized that the concept of "fairness" is not the same as the concept of "equal results." Our minds grasped the idea that "fairness" requires justification and not simple division. Wow!! The problem question which we were trying to generate would be like the concept of fairness in that we needed to realize that to answer the question would require our being able to offer justification, but not just any justification, but justification using MORE IDEAS from areas of ideology, philosophy, etc. We reflected on what we did (our practice) and will change our approach to doing something based on our own insights.

To be able to reflect on practice and change approaches based on own insights is one of the proficiencies expected of candidates in the College of Education's Institutional Standards. The college maintains that mastery of this proficiency is evidence of being a reflective inquirer.

What do the State (FEAP's) standard require? The standards require that a candidate:

Accomplished Practice #2: Communication – uses effective communication: active listening; constructive feedback; individual and group inquiry strategies.

Accomplished Practice #3: Continuous Improvement – engages in lifelong learning and self-reflection: demonstrates respect for diverse perspectives, ideas, and options; works as a member of a learning community; learns from peers; shows evidence of self-reflection.

Accomplished Practice # 4 Critical Thinking – utilizes critical understanding of educational thought and practice: shows ability to think critically and creatively; uses higher-order thinking skills.

Accomplished Practice #6 Ethics – habits that render intelligent professional conduct: demonstrates moral sensibilities: exhibits moral attributes essential for effective professional practice.

What did WE come to know, be able to do or be disposed toward in LEARNING OBJECTIVE #1 that is representative of what the standard calls for?

Learning Objective #1: To formulate a moral, philosophical problem question, and prepare a brief written introduction to the problem question by contrasting the pros and cons in the problem and by laying out the paper's components.

Learning is doing and undergoing the consequences and reflecting on the change. Our professor asked us to divide money equally among some class members, and we did. He then asked us to divide the same amount of money fairly, and we hesitated. Why did we hesitate? Suddenly, as we reflected we realized that the concept of "fairness" is not the same as the concept of "equal results." Our minds grasped the idea that "fairness" requires justification and not simple division. Wow!! The problem question which we were trying to generate would be like the concept of fairness in that we needed to realize that to answer the question would require our being able to offer justification, but not just any justification, but justification using MORE IDEAS from areas of ideology, philosophy, etc. We reflected on what we did (our practice) and will change our approach to doing something based on our own insights. To be able to reflect on practice and change approaches based on own insights is one of the proficiencies expected of candidates by the

State of Florida in the Florida Educator Accomplished Practice #4 – shows ability to think critically.

What do the NBPTS standards require? The standard(s) require from a candidate:
Meaningful Applications of Knowledge – The accomplished teacher understands how subjects he/she studies can be used to explore important issues in their lives.
Reflection – The accomplished teacher regularly analyzes, evaluates and strengthens the quality of his/her practice.

What did WE come to know, be able to do or be disposed toward in LEARNING OBJECTIVE #1 that is representative of what the standard calls for?
Learning Objective #1: To formulate a moral, philosophical problem question, and prepare a brief written introduction to the problem question by contrasting the pros and cons in the problem and by laying out the paper's components.
Learning is doing and undergoing the consequences and reflecting on the change. Our professor asked us to divide money equally among some class members, and we did. He then asked us to divide the same amount of money fairly, and we hesitated. Why did we hesitate? Suddenly, as we reflected we realized that the concept of "fairness" is not the same as the concept of "equal results." Our minds grasped the idea that "fairness" requires justification and not simple division. Wow!! The problem question which we were trying to generate would be like the concept of fairness in that we needed to realize that to answer the question would require our being able to offer justification, but not just any justification, but justification using MORE IDEAS from areas of ideology, philosophy, etc. We reflected on what we did (our practice) and will change our approach to doing something based on our own insights.
To be able to reflect on practice and change approaches based on own insights is one of the proficiencies expected of educators in the National Board for Professional Teaching Standards. The National Board expects accomplished educators to strengthen the quality of his/her practice through reflection.

To work as a group on the educational journey cannot be left to chance (Blair, n.d.). First, I turn to the literature on group development and show class members that they will be moving through five stages of group development. According to Tuckman (n.d.), there are four basic stages of group development: Stage 1 is the forming stage when group members' behavior is driven by a need to be accepted, and to avoid conflict; Stage 2 is the storming stage when initial conflicts begin to emerge; Stage 3 is the norming stage when the rules of engagement for the group become established; and Stage 4 is the performing stage that is characterized by interdependence and flexibility. Tuckman (n.d.) also describes a fifth stage that is the disengagement stage when the group members are proud of having achieved much and proud to be part of the group. I also get class members to understand that each group, or learning community, to be successful must attend to the managerial tasks of the group, and to the interpersonal tasks with regard to the manners and behavior the group will expect from a member in order for the individual to remain a member (Blair, n.d.). .

Now class members should be coming to the realization that on the journey they will produce an argumentative paper as evidence of their learning, and they will do so in learning communities, that is, small groups. I help them to see that there will also be related tasks that might be subsumed under the category of class participation activities, but are critical to the overall course learning task. As a result, three major aspects of course performance emerge: (1) the course artifact, the argumentative paper, (2) group performance, and (3) class participation activities. It is these three elements of the course on which class members' performance will be assessed.

The literature is clear with regard to the use of rubrics to assess candidates' performance (Peat, 2008; Stevens & Levi, 2005). Consequently, I use the second introductory session to introduce class members to the criteria I will use to judge their performance. These criteria are rubrics for the argumentative paper, group performance and class participation. I also share with them the written final course evaluations that I will provide each class member. These final course evaluations (see examples below) highlight, in particular, my assessment of their demonstrating the habits of mind.

Final Course Evaluation/Argumentative Paper
The group paper shows evidence of the problem being defined and introduced. That is, the group shows good evidence of a critical eye toward ideas, i.e., being analytical, thoughtful and reflective, and investigative in clearly defining and introducing a moral, philosophical problem. The group shows good evidence of systematically working, by extending maximum effort, to broaden the knowledge base for the problem, i.e., using research information effectively (i.e., striving for accuracy) to write a comprehensive literature review on the group's problem question; and being inquisitive by going after material with some direction. There is good evidence of the group thinking about its own thinking through the use of reasoning skills to structure arguments. The group shows good evidence of deliberateness and open mindedness in being thoughtful in the use of ideas to justify a position on a problem, ideologically and philosophically. There is good evidence of the group using knowledge acquired in arguments to ground recommendations for change in schooling realities (reflective thoughtfulness: applying past knowledge to new situation(s) and thinking about own thinking). The group's evidence of striving for accuracy by providing a comprehensive bibliography of relevant sources and exactness in APA citations in the narrative and reference section is blemished by a few missing page numbers for quotes in the narrative. The group shows good evidence of thinking and communicating with clarity and precision by exhibiting command of the language and correct use of grammar and syntax.
Performance assessment: Outstanding (2.8)

Final Course Evaluation/Group Performance
XXXX adopted a critical eye toward ideas and actions by inquiring into educational problems and dilemmas. She demonstrated her commitment to being open-minded by

recognizing the wholeness and distinctiveness of other people's ways of experiencing and making meaning during group discussions. She managed impulsivity in group discussions by withholding judgment until understanding was achieved and by being thoughtful in her actions. She was consistent in her focus on her work, and worked to see the project through to its conclusion by employing systematic methods to complete the argumentative paper. She did wonder about why she was doing what she was doing by planning for, reflecting on, and evaluating the quality of her own thinking skills and strategies. She must take time to check over work before submitting final paper because she is more interested in excellent work than in expedience. She showed, although not always, evidence of thinking and communicating with clarity and precision by supporting statements in both written and oral communication. She worked to abstract meaning from one experience and carry it forward and apply it to a new and novel situation by calling upon her store of knowledge and experiences as sources of data to solve new challenges in the group and in group work. . She was curious, and enthusiastic about learning, and inquiry, and mastering her work. . She was generally comfortable in situations where the outcomes were not immediately known and which called for her acting on the basis of adventurous initiative and not just from needing a script. She thought in concert with others and was sensitive to the needs of others and therefore was cooperative and a team member. She held in abeyance, most of the time, her own values, judgments, opinions, and prejudices in order to listen to and entertain the thoughts of others by caring about others and listening well.
Performance assessment: Outstanding (2.8)

Final Course Evaluation/Class Participation
XXXX participated in 92% of the formal class sessions (attendance). She showed evidence of being open-minded; of reflective thoughtfulness; of being curious; of being passionate about her learning; of thinking in concert with others and working with others. She must work more toward grammatical correctness. She did show to some degree evidence of acquiring insights in the class focus discussions. She demonstrated mastery of course content (striving for accuracy) by answering 73% of the multiple-choice items based on the course content; she retook the quiz and improved her score to 91%. She showed some evidence, although not consistently, of an investigative manner in completing class tasks. Her search strategy skills need improvement. She did not show good evidence of being self-evaluative and of transferring knowledge in his/her work on his/her habits of mind inventory (thinking about own thinking and applying past knowledge to new situations).
Performance assessment: Adequate to Outstanding (2.7)

I let class members know that feedback is critical to their learning. As a result, there will be major points on the educational journey at which class members will share work in progress and receive feedback from me. I will use the "track changes" feature in Microsoft Word to facilitate my feedback on the documents they share with me.

Finally, I use the minute paper again at the end of the second introductory session to get class members to reflect. I ask each class member, therefore, to list three things he/she learned from the session about the educational journey in EDF 6608, and to state something that he/she still does not understand about the educational journey.

Learning Objective 1

The goal for the Learning Objective 1 session is to bring candidates to the realization that:

> The educational aim in the course is to create a "thoughtful" and "caring" learning environment in which candidates will grow by deepening and broadening themselves as they work in learning communities, pursuing social ends (the improvement of educational conditions), using ideological, philosophical, sociological, and historical knowledge and thinking skills, so that candidates come to accept the assumption that educative environments induce certain kinds of intellectual, emotional and social dispositions (habits of mind), and as such these habits of mind will be manifested in the class sessions, course tasks, and learning communities. The class is, therefore, structured so that the teacher and students can identify a genuine problem for each learning community, use the curriculum (social foundations) to investigate, discover, and defend solutions to these problems, and as a result, establish connections with the course subject matter.

So:

> Each learning community, therefore, will focus on a specific question it cares about, and then study and resolve it through employing the ideas, the logic, the methods, and the materials of the social, historical and philosophical foundations of education curriculum. The basic pedagogical assumption in the course is that talking with others can yield meaning, knowledge and wisdom and can form requisite dispositions of moral sensibility, and pedagogical thoughtfulness (Hansen, 2001).

The specific learning objective, however, is for each formed learning community (small group) to identify its moral/philosophical problem question and to work on introducing the problem in the introduction section of the argumentative paper. I specify that each group must share its work in progress on the foregoing (using the template for the argumentative paper) with me for my feedback no later 11:30pm on the night of the next class session. This becomes the first major feedback point on the educational journey.

This learning objective is contained in one class session, so I commence the session by asking class members to look back at their feedback from the previous session: things learned from that session about the educational journey, and things that they still do not understand about the educational journey. My pedagogical action takes into account the critical nature of feedback in enhancing my teaching and candidates' learning. According to Hattie and Tiperley (2007) feedback information is provided by some agent with regard to the person's and another's performance or understanding, and usually occurs after instruction that is intended to provide knowledge, skills or to develop dispositions. My use of candidates' feedback enhances my understanding vis-à-vis my pedagogical methods and of candidates' learning. It enables me to close any gaps of misunderstanding on the part of class members. It also serves as a means to get class members to link what might have occurred in the last session to learning in the current and/or future sessions.

What must candidates know, be able to do, and be disposed toward in Learning Objective 1, the first major point on the educational journey? How will their performance be monitored and assessed, that is, what assessments for learning will be used? I help class members see the answers to the foregoing in the visual below.

Learning Objective 1	Content	Skills	Habits of Mind	Assessments for Learning
Given a working prompt by the instructor, candidates working in learning communities will, through consensus, formulate a moral, philosophical problem question in the field of education and using a template provided by the instructor prepare a brief written introduction to the problem question by contrasting the pros and cons in the problem and by laying out the paper's components (synthesis).	Ethical vision of education (ideas and their significance; meaning and necessity of philosophy of education. Kinds of questions.	Group process skills – managerial (mechanisms by which community acts as a unit and not as a loose rabble) and interpersonal (basic manners). Brainstorming – thinking outside the box.	[1] Being investigative and adopting a critical eye toward ideas and actions; [3] Being thoughtful and reflective; *[9] Bringing a freshness of mind to bear on issues, problems, concerns;* *[10] Acting on the basis of own heart and will rather than in ways that are scripted by forces not of own making;* *[11]Demonstrating teamwork*	Assessment of understanding through oral questioning. Assessment of skills through observations and checklists. Assessment of habits of mind through HoM Inventory and self-assessment.

Content Learning: I adhere to Dewey's admonition to "give the pupils something to do, and not something to learn," and ask class members to explore the question, "Is there a difference between facts, information, and ideas?" The guided discussion helps class members to realize that (a) only ideas can lead to change, (b) facts and information serve as a resource for thinking and acquiring ideas, (c) we cannot give another ideas like facts and information, and (d) ideas arise from wrestling with conditions, situations, etc., and working one's way forward. To dramatize the concept of ideas, I take three dollar bills out of my pocket and give them to a class member. I then ask two other class members to join the class member with the money. I then ask the person with the dollar bills (3), to divide them equally among him/herself and the other two group members. Once that is done, usually quite quickly, I ask that the bills be returned to the class member who had them originally, and I ask that class member to now divide the dollar bills among him/herself and the other two class members, fairly. This request usually creates some hesitancy on the part of the class member with the dollar bills, but is followed by the class member offering some verbal criteria for his/her way of allocating the funds. I use this as a teachable moment, and point out that my request to allocate equally met no hesitancy while my request to allocate fairly did. I question class members as to why, and they draw the insight that the latter request did require the use of some criteria beyond simple division, and furthermore, the latter request rested upon the idea of fairness. To stimulate further thinking about the idea of fairness, I ask class members if they realized that the idea of fairness is embedded in the 14th Amendment to the U. S. Constitution, and that the idea helps to guide fair treatment for special needs children in education. Any flashes of light that go on for class members reinforce David Hansen's notion that every idea is a new discovery, and even more so, his poignant insight that "Ideas and the thinking that give rise to them constitute a fundamental aspect of education" (Hansen, 2007, p. 4). I link this insight to the model of learning for our educational journey:

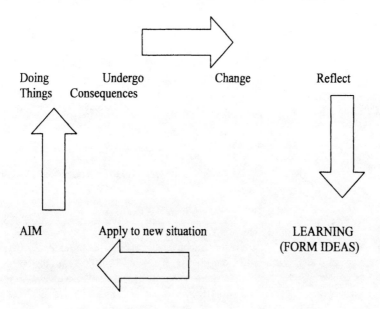

Doing   Undergo   Change   Reflect
Things   Consequences

AIM   Apply to new situation   LEARNING
                                             (FORM IDEAS)

While ideas are transformative, they also have moral implications in terms of the normative, what ought to be. I draw class members into a dialogue about this through (1) the premise that "since ideas matter for the conduct of life [how we ought to live] it is wise to put forward the most ethical and empowering ideas possible" (Hansen, 2007, p. 6), and (2) that how life ought to be lived must be guided by a mature educational philosophy (Hansen, 2007). To make this point, I ask each class member to respond to the following question: "In teaching and learning, what should come first, the subject matter or the student's interest?" I get the class members to see that no matter their answer (their normative judgment as opposed to a descriptive judgment), it is grounded in some philosophical assumptions about reality and how we come to know, and moral theory of what is good conduct (how we ought to live). Class members then get to see that the moral is concerned with what is good conduct, while the ethical is about the evaluation of actions and social rules that regulate conduct, including rules that address actions that are right or wrong. I also bring to their attention that:

> The implied impartiality of moral statements accounts at least in part for their power. If a moral statement were merely expression of my own interest, others would have no reason to pay any special attention to it. After all, my interests and yours might not be the same. But, if a moral judgment is genuinely impartial, it stands to reason that you should pay attention to what I say, because you should make the same judgment in the same circumstances (Harris, p. 10 as cited in "What is Morality," n.d., para. 13).

So, the kind of moral, philosophical question that each learning community (small group) will pursue cannot be (1) a question with one definitive answer that comes from some specific piece of information nor (2) a personal preference that cannot be assessed and is simply an opinion. Instead, a moral, philosophical question requires one to first consider competing questions, and second, evidence and reasoning within multiple systems within which they may be better and worse answers and requires judgment.

It is at this point that I turn to a form of a focused listing exercise by asking each class member to state the most important thing or things that he/she has heard and/or learned about the ethical and the moral in education.

Skills to be acquired: By this third class session, I have been able to organize class members into learning communities (small groups comprised of 2 to 6 class members based on field of study affiliation (e.g., Educational Leadership, Higher Education, International/Intercultural Education, and so on). However, the skills needed for good group function (managerial and interpersonal) are just as critical as content knowledge and process skills. The learning communities I form are at the forming stage, so I remind them of the indicators of that stage as articulated by Tuckman (n.d.):

> Individual behavior is driven by a desire to be accepted by others, and avoid controversy or conflict. Serious issues and feelings are avoided, and people focus on being busy with

routines, such as team organization, who does what, when to meet, etc. But individuals are also gathering information and impressions – about each other, and about the scope of the task and how to approach it. This is a comfortable stage to be in, but the avoidance of conflict and threat means that not much actually gets done.

In addition, I also remind them of Gerard Blair's contention that the first responsibility of a group is to clarify its mission, and the second is to attend to the following basic interpersonal manners:

-encourage everyone to speak out and contribute; ask "the loud-mouth" to summarize, and then ask for other views
-record decisions made so everyone may see that all criticisms must focus on task and not on personality
-Praise progress on the task (if anyone does something well, praise it)
-Debate opposing views held in the group to better understand it (them)
-Realize that first ideas are not always best; generated alternatives and evaluated them in light of the task.

I provide each learning community (small group) with a check list and request that each group complete it at the end of the class session. The check list addresses group managerial and interpersonal skills.

I also bring into play the aspect of class routines through the groups. Ritchhart (2002) contends that

Routines clearly play an important role in ordering and structuring the lives of the group of individuals coexisting in the small space known as a classroom....the importance of routines extends beyond a managerial function. By specifying the guidelines by which learning interactions take place, routines act as a major enculturating force communicating the values of a classroom. Routines not only give a classroom a sense of order and smoothness but also contribute to its unique feel as an environment for learning (p. 86).

I, therefore, ask each group to choose its first coordinator (I have them rotate the role of coordinator throughout the journey), and request that the coordinator provide a class attendance list of group members at the end of each class session.

The opportunity for each group to use the Check List emerges in the group's effort to start working collaboratively to identify a moral, philosophical problem question to guide the group's learning on the educational journey. To help each learning community with that work, I ask the class to first think of the difference between "the what is" and "the what ought to be," and I suggest that a problem needs index might be created by viewing "the what is" minus "the what ought to be" as leading to a problem needs index. I reintroduce the class to the task in the first introductory class session where I asked class members to identify an educational practice or policy that they believed would improve some aspect of education for teachers, or students, or administrators, or counselors, and so on), and provide a brief justification for the practice or policy by using the prompt "This practice or policy ought to occur because...." I get the class to realize that in that exercise it was dealing with "the what is" and "the what ought to be." So, the members in each learning community might start their work on framing a moral/philosophical problem question by first sharing the ways of life in schools today group members find problematic (that is, are they things going on now in schools that go against how they think life ought to be lived in schools?). The group dialogue should then move to the members identifying values that they think should exemplify how life ought to be lived in schools; what would they see going on if life were lived the way they think it ought to? Finally, each group would use the things going on now that go against how the group thinks life ought to be lived in schools and frame a moral, philosophical problem question. The question would start with the word "Should."

To facilitate the brainstorming activity, I share what I call a brainstorming prompt, with the class.

Brainstorming Prompt

What is?	What Ought to Be?	Moral/Philosophical Problem Question

I provide an example of the prompt used previously:

Brainstorming Prompt

What is?	What Ought to Be?	Moral/Philosophical Problem Question
Educational Policy The No Child Left Behind Act requires children in special education to pass tests designed for children without disabilities	To be fair, children with disabilities should not be required to take the tests designed for children without disabilities	Should children with disabilities be required to pass tests designed for children without disabilities?
Educational Policy The No Child Left Behind Act treats children as products to be tested, measured and made more uniform	Education should help children develop their gifts and realize their promise – intellectually, physically, socially and ethically Each child should be seen as being unique and whose growth follows a developmental process	Should educational policies in a democracy contribute to increasing uniformity and standardization or to enriching the development of individuals for social ends?

And, I provide some examples of problem questions developed by learning communities in previous courses:

- Should the kind of education one receives be directly linked to one's location on the social stratification ladder in society? (Urban Education Learning Community).
- Should high-stakes testing be the litmus test for determining effective teaching and learning? (Elementary Education, Physical Education, Reading, Early Childhood Learning Community).
- Should public schools facilitate the acquisition of a bilingual education for students or should they simply be supportive of English acquisition only as mandated in the No Child Left Behind Act of 2001? (TESOL Learning Community).

Each learning community based on the foregoing work drafts the introduction section of its Argumentative Paper on the Argumentative Paper Template and shares its work in progress for my feedback no later than 11:30pm on the day of the next class session which is one week later.

I end the session on Learning Objective 1 by asking class members to start the process of monitoring their growth on the educational journey through reflective action. First, on an individual basis, they must review the habits of mind that were identified at the start of the learning objective as being relevant to enhancing their learning.

-[1] Being investigative and adopting a critical eye toward ideas and actions *Asked questions to fill in the gap between what is known and what is not known; Posed questions about alternative positions or points of view; Probed into the causes of things or just accepted things as they were; Posed questions that required a yes or no answer or posed more complex questions.*

-[3] Being thoughtful and reflective [*Acted and then thought or thought before acting; Strived to clarify and understand what he/she heard and read, etc?; Jumped to offer an opinion about something that he/she did not understand fully; Considered different possibilities before taking action; Accepted the first idea that came to mind.*

-[9] Bringing a freshness of mind to bear on issues, problems, concerns [*Was turned on about learning new things; Liked things that required hard thinking; Was curious about ordinary things; Was interested in inquiring into how and why things are; Wanted to master what he/she had to do.*

-[10] Acting on the basis of own heart and will rather than in ways that are scripted by forces not of own making [*Went beyond established limits; Was comfortable in situations whose outcome were not immediately clear; Accepted failure as part of his/her own growth; Accepted setbacks as challenging and growth producing; Knew when to take educated risks and when not to take impulsive risks; Took a chance in the moment or only after he/she had calculated all costs; Only knew the correct answer or was challenged by the process of finding the answer.*

-[11]Demonstrating teamwork [*Drew energy from others and sought reciprocity; Preferred solitary work; Was sensitive to the needs of others; Was a job hog; just wanted to do things only with him/herself; Let others do all the work for him/her; Was excited about having to justify and test his/her ideas on others; Was willing to accept feedback from a critical friend.*

Then, each class member must go to the Habits of Mind Inventory Template and record his/her reflections vis-à-vis his/her conduct on each of the above habits of mind for Learning Objective 1. I provide the class the prompts below to help class members guide their reflective writing:

Description of Activity for Reflective Analysis
Does the reflection describe a specific activity, its circumstances, situations, or issues (e.g., who was involved? What were the circumstances, concerns or issues involved? When did the event occur? Where did the event occur?)
Analysis of Activity
Does the reflection provide any insight as to why the activity occurred the way it did, and how the way it occurred may or may not be related to learning in the course?
Appraisal of Activity
Does the reflection provide an interpretation of the experience (e.g., is there any use of educational theory and practice?)
Reflection
Does the reflection provide any insights gained from the experience, and does it show how thoughtfulness might have improved as a result of the experience?

To ascertain whether class members' learning in Learning Objective 1 is consistent with institutional, state and professional standards, I ask members of each group to engage in collective reflection about what was learned, and then record the group's consensus in the Meeting Standards Template vis-à-vis its learning in Objective 1 as it relates to the College of Education, Institutional Standards; to the State of Florida's Educator Accomplished Standards; and to the National Board for Professional Standards (see Meeting Standards Template in Appendix).

The individual reflections in the Habits of Mind Inventory, and the group reflections in the Meeting Standards Template must be shared with me for my feedback no later than 11:30pm the day of the next class session.

I conclude this session by (1) asking class members to respond to the following questions "What was our learning Objective for this class session?" and "Did we accomplish the objective?" and (2) by previewing Learning Objective 2. I inform class members that Learning Objective 2 will help them understand the basic structure for writing a literature review on the key concepts in the group's moral/philosophical problem question, and I ask each class member to review the Literature Review and APA Reference Style Tutorials on CE6 Blackboard (Learning Modules, Learning Objective #2) and come to the next class session prepared to answer questions about the tutorials.

Learning Objective II

The goal for this learning objective is to get candidates to maintain their focus on their learning as a process of inquiry. Their initial learning in Learning Objective 1 may be seen as the disequilibrium phase of inquiry where they recognized a forked situation in educational policy and practice, and identified a problem based on their experience. That disequilibrium emerged from something in the candidates' educational experience that did not make moral sense. Now, in this module candidates must acquire background knowledge of the problem that is collect data at hand from the literature.

The specific learning objective is for each learning communities to use research information effectively to write a literature review of key concepts in the problem question. This phase of the educational journey may be viewed as the second step of inductive inquiry: Step 1-the occurrence of a problem, and Step 2-observation and inspection of the facts surrounding the problem.

This learning objective is pursued over two sessions. The first session is devoted to helping class members understand a literature review, and how to make correct APA Style citations. The second session enables class members to work with a Reference Librarian on search strategies, and begin drafting the literature review.

Evaluating how well I have enhanced candidates' understanding in the previous class session is necessary. So, I start the session on a literature review by reviewing the goal of the previous session to have each learning community work to identify a moral, philosophical problem question, write an introduction to the problem in the Argumentative Paper Template, and share that work in progress. I share my analysis of class members' feedback on the most important thing or things they heard and/or learned about ideas, the what is and what ought to be, and the moral/ethical, and let class members know whether their feedback indicated that they were aware of the key content ideas. I ask class members about their brainstorming session to identify their moral, philosophical problem question, and I share the indicators of each stage of group development and ask each learning community to pinpoint the indicators that apply to their first group session.

Do any of these indicators apply (Forming Stage)? Members were concerned about the purpose of the group; about what they had to do; about who would lead; and were dependent upon the group leader.

Do any of these indicators apply (Storming Stage)? Members were becoming frustrated; they were feeling some anger toward the leader, other members, and/or the group tasks; and were feeling discouraged.

Do any of these indicators apply (Norming Stage)? Any frustration on the part of members was dissipating; personal satisfaction was increasing among members; and collaborative efforts were beginning to jell.

Do any of these indicators apply (Performing Stage)? Members were eager to be part of the group; individual members felt a sense of autonomy; members were working well together; leadership functions were being shared; and a sense of interdependence was developing.

The feedback from the above provides me with a sense of the stage of development for each learning community, and clues as to the kinds of intervention methods I may have to use to facilitate group development.

I remind class members that they formed and demonstrated certain habits of mind as they worked to achieve the Learning Objective 1 ([1] Being investigative and adopting a critical eye toward ideas and actions; [3] Being thoughtful and reflective; [9] Bringing a freshness of mind to bear on issues, problems, concerns; [10] Acting on the basis of own heart and will rather than in ways that are scripted by forces not of own making; [11]Demonstrating teamwork), and they were monitoring their growth in this area through their individual written reflections in their habits of mind inventories, and their collective learning for this learning objective in the Meeting Standards Template. They were using their experience on which to reflect and draw insights.

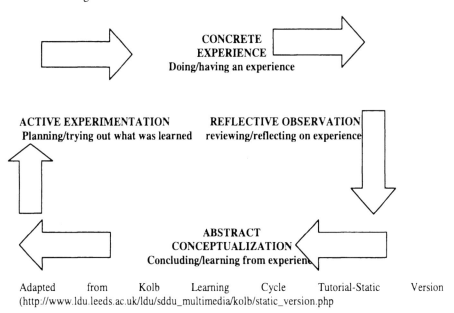

CONCRETE EXPERIENCE
Doing/having an experience

ACTIVE EXPERIMENTATION
Planning/trying out what was learned

REFLECTIVE OBSERVATION
reviewing/reflecting on experience

ABSTRACT CONCEPTUALIZATION
Concluding/learning from experience

Adapted from Kolb Learning Cycle Tutorial-Static Version (http://www.ldu.leeds.ac.uk/ldu/sddu_multimedia/kolb/static_version.php

I inform candidates that it will be important for them to get my feedback on their performance after Learning Objective 1 on their work in progress on the argumentative paper, their group performance, and class participation, and that I would be sharing my feedback after I had reviewed the work that was shared on Objective 1, and that my feedback would be based on the relevant areas in the rubrics for the paper, group performance and class participation.

Argumentative Paper (Collective Work)

Performance criteria	Target/outstanding (3)	Acceptable/Adequate (2)	Unacceptable/inadequate (1)
Construct a moral/philosophical problem and lay out an introduction to that problem	Shows outstanding evidence of a critical eye toward ideas, i.e., being analytical, thoughtful and reflective, and investigative, in clearly defining and introducing a moral, philosophical problem	Shows good evidence of a critical eye toward ideas, i.e., being analytical, thoughtful and reflective, and investigative, and investigative, in clearly defining and introducing a moral, philosophical problem	Shows little evidence of a critical eye toward ideas, i.e., being analytical, thoughtful and reflective, and investigative, in clearly defining and introducing a moral, philosophical problem

Group Performance (Individual Member)

Performance criteria	Target/outstanding (3)	Acceptable/Adequate (2)	Unacceptable/inadequate (1)
Inquire into discrepancies in the educational problem(s)	Shows outstanding evidence of adopting a critical eye by inquiring into discrepancies in the educational problem(s).	Shows good evidence of adopting a critical eye by inquiring into discrepancies in the educational problem(s).	Shows little evidence of adopting a critical eye by inquiring into discrepancies in the educational problem(s).
Thoughtful in actions during group deliberations	Shows outstanding evidence of being thoughtful in his/her actions during group deliberations	Shows good evidence of being thoughtful in his/her actions during group deliberations	Shows little evidence of being thoughtful in his/her actions during group deliberations
Show adventurous initiative	Shows outstanding evidence of acting on the basis of adventurous initiative in his/her learning (taking responsible risks) and not just from needing a script	Shows good evidence of acting on the basis of adventurous initiative in his/her learning (taking responsible risks) and not just from needing a script	Shows little evidence of acting on the basis of adventurous initiative in his/her learning (taking responsible risks) and not just from needing a script

Being curious and passionate about learning	Shows outstanding evidence of being curious and passionate about his/her learning	Shows good evidence of being curious and passionate about his/her learning	Shows little evidence of being curious and passionate about his/her learning
Thought in concert with others	Shows outstanding evidence of thinking in concert with others (thinking interdependently) and being cooperative and a team member	Shows good evidence of thinking in concert with others (thinking interdependently) and being cooperative and a team member	Shows little evidence of thinking in concert with others (thinking interdependently) and being cooperative and a team member

Class Participation (Individual Member)

Performance criteria	Target/outstanding (3)	Acceptable/Adequate (2)	Unacceptable/inadequate (1)
Questioning and Posing problems	Shows outstanding evidence of an investigative manner in class tasks	Shows good evidence of an investigative manner in class tasks	Shows little evidence of an investigative manner in class tasks
Persisting	Shows outstanding evidence of being focused in his/her work on his/her habits of mind inventory and of working to see the projects through to completion	Shows good evidence of being focused in his/her work on his/her habits of mind inventory and of working to see the projects through to completion	Shows little evidence of being focused in his/her work on his/her habits of mind inventory and field work and of working to see the projects through to completion
Thinking about own thinking Applying past knowledge to new situations	Shows outstanding evidence of being self-evaluative and transfer of knowledge in his/her work on his/her habits of mind inventory	Shows good evidence of being self-evaluative and transfer of knowledge in his/her work on his/her habits of mind inventory	Shows little evidence of being self-evaluative and transfer of knowledge in his/her work on his/her habits of mind inventory

I use another "minute paper" feedback request here by asking class members to do the following: (1) Name something each class member felt he/she learned from Learning Objective 1 that contributed to his/her producing the problem question and introduction to his/her group's introduction to the argumentative paper, and (2) Name something about which he/she is not clear still with regard to his/her completing the introduction to the group's argumentative paper.

I then turn to Learning Objective II:

Learning Objective II	Content	Skills	Habits of Mind	Assessments for Learning
After a presentation by the instructor on literature review, and participating in an information inquiry and research strategies session with a Reference Librarian, candidates in their learning communities will use research information effectively to write a literature review of key concepts in the problem question (application).	Know what a literature review is. Know basic APA citation requirements. Search strategy techniques–know about keywords, synonyms, Boolean, truncation, adjacency, subject headings/descriptors; Know about relevant databases; Know about search tools; Know about criteria to evaluate quality of web resources; Know if library owns something;	Be able to write a literature review using APA and electronic technologies. Demonstrate group process skills - managerial (mechanisms by which community acts as a unit and not as a loose rabble) and interpersonal (basic manners). Brainstorming – thinking outside the box. Group process skills – managerial (mechanisms by which community acts as a unit and not as a loose rabble) and interpersonal (basic manners).	[1] Being investigative and adopting a critical eye toward ideas and actions; [3] Being thoughtful and reflective; [4] Being focused and systematic; [6] Striving for accuracy (exactness and correctness); *[7] Thinking and communicating with clarity and precision; [11] Demonstrating teamwork*	Assessment of understanding through Pre-Post- Quiz. Assessment of skills through observations and checklists. Assessment of habits of mind through HoM Inventory and self-assessment.

I use the Think/Pair/Share technique to help class members attend to what a literature review is. Based on their review of a Literature Review Tutorial https://lms.fiu.edu/webct/urw/lc1576119463011.tp1576152166051/RelativeResourceMan ager/Template/Literature%20Review%20in%20the%20Social%20Sciences.mht;JSES-SIONID=Tjn9K8mM1hTfkjJwhVXvjR1PQVJhHWQMymzQPC9W4Vt1rWnLcwC1!-1222021331!online10.fiu.edu!80!-1!977104280!online16.fiu.edu!80!-1!1249650220402 I ask class members to think about and make individual notes about the following questions: (1) What is the purpose of a literature review? (2) What is a peer reviewed journal, and what is its relevance for your literature review? (3) What is the difference between a primary and a secondary source, and what is the relevance for your literature review? (4) How does a literature review differ from a research paper? And (5) What does "empirical" mean, and what is the relevance for your literature review? I then ask them to join their respective groups (pair) and discuss their responses to the questions for about 15 minutes, at the end of which I call on different groups to share their answers with the entire class. During this sharing I take the opportunity to point out any class members' misunderstandings.

I repeat the technique for class members' review of the tutorial on APA Reference Style. This time I ask class members to think about the following uses of APA and pair by their groups and decide whether the use is correct or incorrect:

Direct quotation
Perrin (2004) argues that "the research process is a complex combination of thinking, searching, reading, evaluating, writing and revising" (p. 1).

Indirect quotation
It is crucial to evaluate the sources when you quote from the Internet in your research pa-per (Perrin, 2004).

Citations from a secondary source
Samovar and Porter (as cited in Peterson, 2002, para.3) discuss that language
    must be first understood as symbols.

References citation
Perrin, Robert. (2004). *Pocket guide to APA style*. Boston: Houghton Miffin Company.

Book chapter
Roll, W.P. (1976). ESP and memory. In J.M.O. Wheatley & H.L. Edge (Eds.),
    Philosophical dimensions of parapsychology (pp. 154-184). Springfield, IL:American
    Psychiatric Press.

Journal article
Maki, R.H. (1982). Categorization effects which occur in comparative judgment tasks.
    Memory & Cognition, 10, 252-264.

Web site source
Thaller, M. (2007) *Cool cosmos.* Retrieved August 27, 2007, from
    http://coolcosmos.ipac.caltech.edu/

I get groups to share their answers with the entire class, and I help the class with correct re-sponses to the citations. The two exercises enable me and class members to get a sense of the class members' working knowledge of a literature review and APA citations.

On the other hand, to write a literature review requires some knowledge of information search strategies and techniques in order to locate scholarly journal articles and research studies, books, and reports and documents from the Educational Research Information Center (ERIC) or request materials through the InterLibrary Loan system. I employ the assistance of Stephanie Brenenson, a

Reference Librarian at Florida International University, in providing a search strategies work session for class members on the foregoing areas. To ascertain class members' learning from this workshop, I ask class members to complete the following workshop Pre-/Post Quiz that is developed around knowing about keywords, synonyms, boolean, truncation, adjacency, subject headings/descriptors, relevant databases, search tools, criteria to evaluate quality of web resources, if the library owns something, and basic APA citation requirements.

SEARCH STRATEGIES KNOWLEDGE CHECK

Research Topic: Explore the impact of economic status on the academic success of children.

1. Using this research topic, answer the following questions (circle your answer or mark it by highlighting it):

Which of the following lists of keywords best describe the topic?

impact, status, children

economic status, academic success, children

impact, academic success, children

impact, economic status, success

2. You could use any of these synonyms for economic status, but which would be the most helpful for your search?

upper class

middle class

low class

income

3. Which of the following Boolean search statements would work as part of your search?

academic success AND academic achievement

academic success OR academic achievement

academic success NOT academic achievement

none of the above

4. If you truncate the word economic like this "economic?" which of the following would not be included in the results?

economic status

economical

economy

economics

5. Which of the following would not be an accurate use of adjacency?

economic status ADJ academic success

economic ADJ status

academic ADJ success

academic ADJ achievement

6. Which of the following databases would probably be least useful for a search on your topic?

Education database

Newspaper database

Sociology database

Medical database

7. The subject headings/descriptors below come from the full record of a relevant article titled: "Children in Poverty: Trends, Consequences, and Policy Options." Which of the selected descriptors would probably not be useful for your search? DE: Descriptors Academic Achievement; Adjustment (to Environment); *At Risk Persons; Child Development; Child Health; *Children; Demography; Educational Attainment; Low-Income Groups; * Poverty; * Public Policy; Trend Analysis

Academic Achievement

Poverty

Low Income Groups

Child Health

8. If you were searching for a book on your topic in the library, what tool would you use?

Internet

ERIC

Library Catalog

SFX

9. What library service will permit you to order books and articles that are not owned by the library?

Reserve

Circulation

Interlibrary loan

Proxy server

10. Which of the following criteria are important in evaluating the quality of a web resource?

Timeliness/Currency

Authority/Source

Objectivity/Bias

All of the above

11. How would one determine if the FIU Libraries own the following article?

TI: Reading Comprehension Requires Knowledge---of Words and the World

AU: Hirsch, E. D., Jr.

SO: American Educator; v 27 n1 p10-13 Spr 2003

AN: EJ672462

Search the internet

Search a database

Search the Catalog

None of the above

12. According to APA style, which of the following is not a correct way to refer to an idea or statement that is not your own?

A recent comparison of student performance (Hirsch, 12)...

Hirsch (2003) compared student performance...

In a recent study of student performance (Hirsch, 2003)...

In 2003, Hirsch, compared student performance...

13. Which of the following citations is written in APA style?

Hirsch, E. D. (2003). Reading comprehension requires knowledge-of words and the world. *American Educator*, 27 (1), 10-13.

Hirsch, E. D. "Reading Comprehension Requires Knowledge-of Words and the World."
American Educator, 27.1 (2003): 10-13.
Hirsch, E. D. 2003. "Reading Comprehension Requires Knowledge-of Words and the
World." *American Educator* 27 (2003): 10-13.
Hirsch, E. (2003). Reading Comprehension Requires Knowledge-of Words and the
World. *American Educator*, 27 n.1, 10-13.

I conclude this session by asking if any class member has written a literature previously, and I direct those who have not to take a look at the literature review section of the papers completed previously. I also remind the class that the next class session will be held in the Library. The first hour of that session will be devoted to the Search Strategies Workshop conducted by the Reference Librarian, and the remainder of the session will enable each learning community to search for information and to start writing the literature review section of the argumentative paper.

Library Session. This library session reinforces the inductive inquiry focus of the educational journey. Having identified a moral, philosophical problem question, the next step for class members is to inspect the facts related to the problem, that is, engage in information inquiry. Information inquiry is the processes of searching for information and applying information to answer questions. "Questioning is at the core of information inquiry and drives the teaching and learning process. In an era of 'one answer' standardized tests, this idea of opening a student's mind to questioning and exploring many answers is essential" ("Inquiry-Based Learning," n.d., para. 3). The Reference Librarian therefore uses the problem questions generated by each learning community to guide the search strategies learning session. At the end of the search strategies session, each learning community applies its search strategies knowledge to finding relevant information, and using that information to write a literature review on the key concepts in each group's problem question.

Class members continue the process of monitoring their individual growth on the educational journey by reviewing the habits of mind relevant to this learning objective:

-[1] Being investigative and adopting a critical eye toward ideas and actions
Asked questions to fill in the gap between what is known and what is not known; Posed questions about alternative positions or points of view; Probed into the causes of things or just accepted things as they were; Posed questions that required a yes or no answer or posed more complex questions.
-[3] Being thoughtful and reflective;
Acted and then thought or thought before acting; Strived to clarify and understand what he/she heard and read, etc?; Jumped to offer an opinion about something that he/she did not understand fully; Considered different possibilities before taking action; Accepted the first idea that came to mind.
[4] Being focused and systematic;
Stuck to tasks until they were completed or gave up easily; Set up a systematic system to guide his/her completing tasks; Gave up easily when the answer to something was not

immediately known; Stayed on focus throughout the learning experience or was easily distracted.
-[6] Striving for accuracy (exactness and correctness);
Worked to produce excellent work; Checked over what he/she produced; Worked to perfect his/her work; Held to high standards any work he/she produced.
-[7] Thinking and communicating with clarity and precision;
Was clear in his/her writing and speaking; Used fuzzy language and thinking; Used precise language and defined terms and ideas clearly; Used good thinking skills and logic.
-[11] Demonstrating teamwork.
Drew energy from others and sought reciprocity; Preferred solitary work; Was sensitive to the needs of others; Was a job hog; just wanted to do things only with him/herself; Let others do all the work for him/her; Was excited about having to justify and test his/her ideas on others; Was willing to accept feedback from a critical friend.

Each class member writes his/her reflections on the above in his/her Habits of Mind Inventory, and then works with his/her group members to reflect on their learning in Learning Objective II to ascertain whether their learning is consistent with institutional, state and professional standards. Each group writes its collective reflection about what was learned in the Meeting Standards Template. The individual reflections in the Habits of Mind Inventory and the group reflections in the Meeting Standards Template, plus the work in progress on the Argumentative Paper (Introduction, Literature Review-in progress, References-in progress) are shared with me for my feedback no later than 11:30pm the day of the next class session.

Now that each group has been working on multiple occasions, I try to ascertain two group development things from each group: (1) what are the things contributing to good group development, and (2) what are the things that are inhibiting good group development. I share this feedback with the class, and I use it to zero in on if group intervention with any group is needed on my part.

Learning Objective III

While the goal of inquiry in Learning Objective 1 was linked to the disequilibrium phase of inquiry where a forked situation was recognized, and the goal in Learning Objective 2 was linked to the inquiry phase of acquiring background knowledge of the problem, the goal of inquiry in this Learning Objective 3 is the formation of hypotheses and the elaboration those hypotheses through reasoning.

The specific learning objective here is for each learning community to first proffer an hypothesis with regard to its problem question, and then sketch/structure an argument to be used to justify the learning community's position.

This learning objective is covered in one session. I start this session by using the feedback from groups about things that are contributing to and things that are inhibiting good group development to share my observations about where each group is on its stage of development. At this point in the journey, each group should be past the forming and storming stages and exhibiting characteristics of the norming stage (the rules of group operation should have been established; the group's tasks clear; group members understand each other better and appreciate each others' skills and experience, and feel part of a cohesive group). Each group has the opportunity to respond to my feedback, and to clarify any misinterpretations. If needed, I enact group interventions to resolve managerial or interpersonal problems.

I engage the class in a review of what has been done so far on the educational journey in Learning Objective 1, and Learning Objective II, solicit reflective insights so far, and then I focus the class on Learning Objective III.

Learning Objective III	Content	Skills	Habits of Mind	Assessments for Learning
After presentations by the instructor, candidates in learning communities will sketch/structure argument(s) for the community's argumentative paper (application).	Know the kinds of arguments Know the forms of arguments.	Be able to check the validity of an argument. Be able to justify an argument. Demonstrate group process skills - managerial (mechanisms by which community acts as a unit and not as a loose rabble) and interpersonal (basic manners).	*[3] Being thoughtful and reflective* [5] Thinking about own thinking *[11] Demonstrating teamwork.*	Assessment of understanding through constructed response questions. Assessment of skills through constructed response questions and checklists. Assessment of habits of mind through HoM Inventory and self-assessment.

Learning Objective III enhances the logic of inquiry (Dewey, 1938b). This objective helps candidates to move from the observed conditions, the facts of the problem in Learning Objective II, to hypothesize what will happen, the idea stage. This suggested forecast with regard to the problem must be examined, however, with the goal of its functional fitness vis-à-vis resolving the problem. This examination is done through reasoning. Whether the hypothesis actually functions is determined later when it is put into operation.

So, I ask each learning community to take a position on its problem question. This position forms a working conclusion. I then ask each learning community to either offer a reason or provide some concrete pieces of evidence to support the conclusion.

Content Learning: The results of the foregoing tasks facilitate my inquiring of class members as to what kind of argument each learning community had created. If class members do not know, I help them to see that (1) those groups that offered a reason for their conclusions had created a deductive argument in which the conclusion is based on the truthfulness of the reason(s)-the premise(s), while those groups that provided evidence for their conclusions had created an inductive argument in which the conclusion is probable based on the evidence, and the conclusion goes beyond the evidence-premise(s).

But each learning community needed to know that within each kind of argument (deductive and inductive) there are different forms (for example, within deductive, there are categorical and hypothetical forms, and within inductive, there are enumerative, post hoc, analogy, statistical forms).

Skills to be acquired: To advance this stage of inquiry, class members must understand that they are not testing their hypotheses empirically, that is seeking empirical proof for their hypotheses, but instead are using logic to make inferences, that is provide logical proof. To do so, however, requires the use of the rules of logic, and the use of its most fundamental concept, an argument. While logic will not specify the content of the argument, it tells how to arrange the argument in a logical fashion (structure and validity), and the best way to justify it. Class members learn how to check the validity of deductive and inductive forms of arguments using the matrix below:

Kind of Argument Deductive	Kind of Argument Deductive	Kind of Argument Inductive
Form of argument Categorical	Form of argument Hypothetical	Form of argument Enumeration, Analogy, Causal Connection, Statistical
Validity checks	Validity checks	Validity checks
Four term fallacy; faulty exclusion; undistributed middle; illicit distribution	Affirming the antecedent; denying the antecedent; affirming the consequent; denying the consequent	Sample size; faulty comparison; post-hoc fallacy; questionable statistics

Class members also learn to check for informal fallacies in statements made since statements that appear to be an argument, but are not are fallacious, they are informal fallacies. Informal fallacies are errors in reasoning in particular in statements made. Class members learn to spot the following informal fallacies: *argumentum ad hominem*, appeal to authority, *non-sequitur*, begging the question, complex question, equivocation, ambiguity, appeal to pity, converse accident (fallacy of composition), and accident (fallacy of division).

The learning here to justify an argument in this objective is consistent with John Dewey's idea of "warranted assertability" (Dewey, 1938b). Each learning community is taught how to offer support (justification) for an argument which asserts that certain conditions will result from certain actions, not as timeless truth, but as an outcome for further inquiry. This form of reasoning is best accommodated through a hypothetical form of argument (a conditional claim) in which each learning community argues that if a certain ideological/philosophical proposition holds then a certain consequence should follow (the consequence in this case is the group's position on its problem question). To provide adequate ground for the foregoing, each learning community will draw on ideological, philosophical, social theory and historical ideas to affirm the proposition (the antecedent and its link to the consequent). The warranted assertability regarding the conditional claim will be the group's position on its problem question.

I use the "Compass Points" tool as advocated by Ritchhart & Perkins, 2008) to help class members think about arguments and justification before they offer support for the stand they are taking on their problem question. I ask class members the following four questions: What excites you about offering an argument? What worries you about offering an argument? What additional information would help you offer your argument? What steps might you take to increase your understanding of offering an argument?

Individual class members finally reflect on their demonstration of the habits of mind relevant to this objective, and write their reflections in their Habits of Mind Inventory: [3] Being thoughtful and reflective-did they act and then think, did they think before acting; did they strive to clarify and understand what they heard, read, etc.? Did they jump to offer an opinion about something that they did not fully understand? Did they consider different possibilities before taking action? Did they accept the first idea that came to mind? [5] Thinking about own thinking-Did they plan for, reflect on, and evaluate the quality of their thinking? Were they increasingly aware of their actions on others? Did they develop and use mental maps or rehearsed before they performed an action? Did they reflect on their actions? Did they wonder about why they were doing what they were doing? Did they explain their decision-making processes on matters? [11] Demonstrating teamwork-Did they draw energy from others and sought reciprocity? Did they prefer solitary work? Were they sensitive to the needs of others? Were they job hogs, just wanting to do things only with themselves? Did they let others do all of the work for them? Were they excited about having to justify and test their ideas on others? Were they willing to accept feedback from a critical friend?

Likewise, each learning community links its learning in Learning Objective 3 to meeting specific proficiencies in College, State and Professional Standards in its written reflection in the Meeting Standards Template.

Each learning community then has until 11:30pm of the day of the next class session to share its work in progress through Learning Objective 3 on its (1) Argumentative Paper, (2) Habits of Mind Inventory, and (3) Meeting Standards Template.

At this stage in the educational journey, I provide class members with more performance feedback. I use the criteria for judging performance, the rubrics, and share written assessments for each class member with regard to his/her performance on the argumentative paper, for his/her group performance, and class participation.

I lay the ground work for Learning Objective 4 accordingly. First, I share the learning objective: After participating in a series of analytical focus discussions on ideological and philosophical, sociological, and historical readings assigned by the instructor, candidates in learning communities will use ideas from the readings as support to justify the com-

munity's ideological/philosophical argument vis-à-vis the problem question (application), and then the content knowledge and process skills to acquire: Understand various ideologies and philosophic schools of thought: ideologies of conservatism, liberalism, and schools of thought: idealism (Plato), and pragmatism, progressivism (Dewey); Understand various social theories: functionalist theory, conflict theory, interactionist theory, interpretivist theory and sociological content: conflict theory, education/conflict theory, education/functionalist theory, family/functionalism, family/conflict theory, symbolic interactionism); Understand various historical events in American education (historical content: liberty and literacy; school as a public institution; teaching in a public institution: the professionalization movement; social diversity and differentiated schooling; and school reform)-Group process skills-
managerial (mechanisms by which community acts as a unit and not as a loose rabble) and interpersonal (basic manners). The habits of mind to facilitate application of the knowledge and skills are: Adopting a critical eye toward ideas and actions [1], Seeing things from different perspectives [2], Being thoughtful and reflective [3], Thinking about own thinking [5], Applying past knowledge to new situations [8], Being cooperative [11], and Being attuned and respectful [12]. Assessment of facts and concepts will be checked through multiple-choice questions; assessment of skills through observations and checklists, and assessment of habits of mind through HoM Inventory and self-assessment.

This learning objective runs for seven sessions, and the first of the seven sessions is conducted in the chat room of the online WebCT/Blackboard system. If class members are satisfied with the online environment after the first session, I then continue the second and third of the seven sessions online. Since the research literature suggests that the use of both synchronous and asynchronous environments best accommodate different learning styles, I have the class return to the classroom for the fourth and fifth sessions, and return to the online environment for the final two sessions.

The learning sessions in Learning Objective 4 are framed around David Hansen's idea of the "focused discussion" (Hansen, 2001). The focused discussion draws out the learner by focusing on his/her thinking about key conceptual ideas about education and schooling, and it nurtures the social individual through cooperation and communication with others. It is styled like a Socratic dialogue, encourages participation, and promotes leadership by asking each learning community to take the lead during the discussion of its assigned reading.

Learning Objective IV

The educative experience being facilitated on the educational journey follows the essentials of reflective inquiry. In Learning Objective 1, each learning community focused on a genuine problem that served as the stimulus for further inquiry and thought. In Learning Objective 2, each learning community turned to acquiring background information needed to deal with the problem. In Learning Objective 3, each learning community proffered a working solution that the community was responsible for developing in a logical manner. Now in Learning Objective 4, each community makes its argument and the meaning of the ideas in its solution clearer.

Learning Objective II	Content	Skills	Habits of Mind	Assessments for Learning
After participating in a series of analytical focus discussions on ideological, philosophical, sociological and historical readings assigned by the instructor, candidates in learning communities will use ideas from the readings as support to justify the community's ideological/philosophical argument vis-à-vis the problem question (application).	Understand various ideologies and philosophic schools of thought: ideologies of conservatism, liberalism, and schools of thought: idealism (Plato), and pragmatism, progressivism (Dewey). Understand various social theories. Understand various historical events in American education (historical content: liberty and literacy; school as a public institution; teaching in a public institution: the professionalization movement; social diversity and differentiated schooling; and school reform).	Constructing knowledge through visual tool-graphic organizer

Group process skills - managerial (mechanisms by which community acts as a unit and not as a loose rabble) and interpersonal (basic manners) | *[1] Adopting a critical eye toward ideas and actions;* [2] Seeing different perspectives; [3] Being thoughtful and reflective; *5] Thinking about own thinking;* [8] Applying past knowledge to new situations; [11] Being cooperative; [12] Being attuned and respectful | Assessment of facts, concepts through multiple-choice questions. Assessment of skills through observations and checklists. Assessment of habits of mind through HoM Inventory and self-assessment. |

The support for each group's argument comes from ideas garnered from specific readings. The ideas in the readings deal with the ideologies of traditional conservatism and liberalism, the philosophies of Plato and John Dewey, the social theories of functionalism, conflict theory and symbolic interactionism, and the historical aspects in American education of liberty and literacy, the professionalization of teaching, social diversity and differentiated schooling, and school reform.

To encourage participation and leadership, I assign a reading to each learning community, and ask that the community, after doing its reading, provide its response to the following questions: (1) what is the reading all about? (2) what did the community already know that was contained in the reading? (3) what in the reading does the community want to know more about? The community posts responses to the foregoing questions (online) one week prior to the focused discussion on the reading. This enables all other class members to respond to the community posts (raising more questions and/or clarifying ideas), and provides me the opportunity to stimulate further thinking or direct class members to where in the upcoming focused discussions their inquiries might arise.

I adhere to what the literature says about responsive facilitation and request that during focused discussions class members follow my instructions, do not carry on private conversations, and be prepared to be called upon during the dialogue. I moderate the focused discussions on the readings (online and in the classroom) one week after the community's posting. I use a set of focused questions to frame the Socratic dialogue for each session. The dialogue is intended to help class members make connections between ideas in the reading and the support for their respective arguments. At the end of each focused discussion session, I request that each class member answer, online, the question "what did I learn from the focused discussion?" The process facilitates the K-W-L learning technique, enables me to get a good sense of class members' understanding of the ideas.

Content Learning: I use the following key focus questions to help class members acquire an understanding of each reading:

Subject: The ideology of conservatism. E-book *The Conservative Tradition in America* by Dunn, Charles W.; Woodard, J.David. (1996) chapters 1, 2, 3, 4, 5, 6 and 7 http://www.netLibrary.com/urlapi.asp?action=summary&v=1&bookid=18667
Focus Questions: When did contemporary American conservatism first emerge? Can you name some American conservative and liberal think tanks? Can you identify and explain some of the key assumptions of conservative thought? How do the authors define and distinguish the terms "political culture," and "political ideology"? Are there implications in the definitions for modern day conservatism and liberalism? What severed the classical tradition of Western political thought from its roots and asserted the role of man? How did this influence liberalism and modern American conservatism? What are the classical roots of conservative thought? Do you see any historical development to American conservatism? To what do conservatives attribute the problems in public schools, according to the authors?

Subject: The philosophy of Plato. E-book *The Republic* by Plato (Book VII) http://www.ilt.columbia.edu/publications/digitext.html
Focus Questions: How does Plato use the allegory of the cave to argue that some persons must be educated differently than most others in society? How does Plato argue for jus-

tice and fairness through the concept of the perfect state? How does Plato argue that the dialectic is the best process to pursue truth? How does Plato use the concept of the divided line to argue for distinctions between intellect and opinion?

Subject: The ideology of liberalism. E-book Liberalism *and American Identity* by Garry, Patrick M. (1992) chapters 1, 4, 6, 9
http://www.netLibrary.com/urlapi.asp?action=summary&v=1&bookid=28058
Focus Questions: What does the author mean when he says "Liberal beliefs influenced the birth of America"? Are there implications for the way the following terms such as "democrat," and "republican," are used today? Can you identify and explain some of the assumptions of progressive liberalism? How are classical liberalism and progressive liberalism related? Are there implications for today's Democratic and Republican parties? Who are some liberals who shaped America? What distinctions does the author make between liberalism and conservatism? According to the author, how do progressive liberals approach the following issues; the fight against crime, abortion, and welfare/workfare?

Subject: The philosophy of John Dewey. E-book *Democracy and Education* (1916). Chapters 1-7, 8-15 and 20-26
http://www.ilt.columbia.edu/publications/digitext.html
Focus Questions: Chapters 1-7. How does John Dewey link the concept of "renewal" to the concept of "education"? How does John Dewey link the concept of "bringing up," to the idea of a social community sustaining itself? How does John Dewey build the case for intelligence as being derived from social interaction? Dewey seems to define "Mind" as a mechanism for connecting needs/means to desires/ends in a manner that produces better-desired states. Do you agree? Is the rampant individualism fostered in American society antithetical to Dewey's idea of the democratic ideal?
Focus Questions: Chapters 8-15, and 20-26. To Dewey, the aim of education is "the continued capacity for growth." What does he mean? To Dewey, what is wrong with the following aims of education; the aim of natural development and the aim of social efficiency? How does Dewey answer the following question; In teaching and learning what should come first, the subject matter or the student's interest? What does Dewey mean by Thinking + Knowledge = Inference? How does Dewey view the following dualism; mind/body, subject matter/method, academic/vocational? What does Dewey mean when he says "knowledge comes from inquiry not from being made a disciple of another? What does Dewey mean when he says "dualisms in theories of knowledge lead to dualisms in theories of morals?

Subject: Market ideology versus democratic values. E—book *The Struggle for Control of Public Education: Market Ideology versus Democratic Values,* by Engel, Michael (2000) chapters 1, 2, 3, 4, 5, 6, 7, 8 and 9
http://www.netLibrary.com/urlapi.asp?action=summary&v=1&bookid=51358
Focus Questions: What does the author mean when he says "current day discussions about the future of education are conducted almost entirely in the language of the free market: individual achievement, competition, choice, economic growth and national security"? The author suggests, "market ideology undercuts the basic values of public edu-

cation? Do you agree? Explain. What are some of the assumptions of market ideology, according to the author? What arguments are offered by the author for democracy over market ideology? Why does the author draw on John Dewey to help him make his case? How does the author link the following educational reforms to market ideology: privatization/school choice, educational technology, school to work, and standards?

Subject: Social theories of functionalism, conflict theory and interpretivism. E-book *School and society* by Feinberg, Walter & Soltis, Jonas (1998) Parts 1, 2, 3 and 4.http://www.netLibrary.com/urlapi.asp?action=summary&v=1&bookid=53470
Focus Questions: What are the main ideas underlying the school of thought of the functionalists? What connections are there between the school of thought of the functionalists and the ideology of conservatism? Are the conservative concepts of "the organic society," "the hierarchical principle," "meritocracy," "order/stability," manifested in the social theory of the functionalism? What are the main ideas underlying the school of thought of the conflict theorists? What connections are there between the school of thought of conflict theory and the ideology of Marxism? Is the Marxist concept of "inequitable class relations in society" manifested in the social theory of conflict theory? What are the main ideas underlying the school of thought of the interpretivists? What connections are there between the school of thought of the interpretivists and the ideology of liberalism? Are the liberal concepts of "the collective good," "economic equality," "social change," and "social intelligence" manifested in the social theory of interpretivism?

Subject: Social theories of functionalism, conflict theory/Marxism and symbolic interactionism. E-book *Sociology basics* by Bankston, Carl L. (2000) sociological concepts C - conflict theory, D - democracy, E - education, education/conflict theory, education/functionalist theory, F - family, family/functionalism, family/conflict theory, M - Marxism, S - symbolic interactionism
http://www.netLibrary.com/urlapi.asp?action=summary&v=1&bookid=51646;
Focus Questions: What are the main ideas underlying the social theory of conflict theory? How does conflict theory view and explain education and the family? Are the concepts of Marxism manifested in the way conflict theorists view education and the family? What are the main ideas underlying functional theory? How does functionalist theory view and explain education and the family? What are the main ideas underlying the social theory of symbolic interactionism? How does symbolic interactionism view and explain education and the family?

Subject: History-Liberty and literacy in America (chapters 2 and 9); The professionalization of teaching (chapters 3 and 10); Social diversity and differentiated schooling (chapters 5 and 11); School reform (chapters 7 and 11). In Tozer, S., Violas, P., & Senese, G. (2006). 6th edition. *School and society*. Boston: McGraw-Hill.
Focus Questions: Chapter 2. How does the concept of "democratic localism" epitomize the idea of liberty? Is the underlying ideology manifested that of conservatism or liberalism? Does the structure of the social unit of the family and farm life, and participation in democratic localism determine how literacy is operationalized? Are there specific implications for how school is conducted given the ideas in questions 1, 2 and 3?

Focus Questions: Chapter 9. In contemporary America is literacy tied to social needs and to economic and social advancement in society? Are there implications for social class, ethnic groups, etc.? What are the major differences among conventional literacy, functional literacy, cultural literacy, and critical literacy? How is the value of literacy manifested in schools through conventional literacy, functional literacy, cultural literacy, and critical literacy?

Focus Questions: Chapter 3. Is the idea of "the common school" tied to economic benefits and to the benefits of business? Is the common school model tied to the Prussian model of "compassionate conservatism"? Does this model facilitate a class-based system? How do the common schools promote the development of an industrial morality? What are the implications for schooling vis-à-vis the marriage of Puritanism, industrialization and educational reform?

Focus Questions: Chapter 10. Is the professionalization of teaching guided by the idea of social efficiency or democratic progressivism? Is the professionalization movement in teaching guided by modern liberal ideology of specialized expertise and scientific rationality? Are the school reforms proposed by James Conant and the Holmes and Carnegie Groups grounded in conservative or liberal ideology?

Focus Questions: Chapter 5. How do urbanization, immigration, industrialization, corporate capital industrialism and industrial management [scientific management] all contribute to the bureaucratization of public schools? How are the ideologies of modern conservatism and progressive liberalism manifested in the movements of social efficiency and developmental democracy? Does compulsory schooling facilitate schooling for equal opportunity or for meritocracy?

How does mass schooling impact the idea of how people learn?

Focus Questions: Chapter 7. During the Cold War Era was school reform linked to national security and national interests and social stability? Why are the reforms pushed by the progressive-era new liberalism seen by Bestor, Koerner, Smith, Conant, etc., as diminishing the importance of academic achievement? How is testing in schools seen as identifying innate aptitudes?

Focus Questions: Chapter 11. How are meritocratic versus democratic ideals played out in schools today? Why is the cause of economic problems in contemporary America seen as a failure of the educational system? Does a corporate liberal ideology guide the current contemporary school reform movement?

Is there any connection between the ideology of management and control and the following prominent school reforms: teacher professionalization, computer technology, parent involvement in schools, school-to-work and school choice? Are any of the reforms consistent with the ideology of democratic problem solving and participation?

I help class members to see the link between ideology, philosophy and sociology through the model below:

Philosophy Finding the meaning of life outside the confines of sacred institutions. Reasoning/logic. What Ought to Be.	Theology Finding the meaning of life; the official doc-trine/dogma of sacred institutions. Subordina-tion of reason to faith. What Ought to Be.	Ideology The shared beliefs and values of a group; ex-pressed through views of past, present and policy actions. The Ends to Be Achieved.

Philosophy Plato (Idealism) The perfect state; hierarchy; The divided line; the dialectic; A ruling elite	Traditional Conservatism Edmund Burke The organic society; the hierarchical principle; meritocracy; incremental change and preserving the status quo; respect for order; individual de- fined by authority; divine intent Liberalism John Locke, Rousseau Political freedom; social contract; economic freedom; laissez-faire; social change; rational rule of law; private property and privacy; individual discovers truth; individual defined by self interest; religious beliefs private not a state matter.

Classical Liberalism leads to American modern conservatism and to American Progressive Liberalism.

Early American Conservatism	American Classical Liberalism
Alexander Hamilton, John Adams	Thomas Jefferson, James Madison
Ruling class; political and economic order; centralized government that supports commercial interests; minimize changes not instigated by elite; distrust of experimentation	Political freedom; popular rule; economic freedom; rational intelligence; the individual prior to society; hierarchical principle; natural aristocracy; religious beliefs private; natural rights; progress; social contract

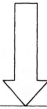

American Modern Conservatism	American Progressive Liberalism
Coolidge, Reagan, G.H. Bush, G.W. Bush	The New Deal-Roosevelt; The Fair Deal-Truman; The Great Society-Johnson
Laissez-faire; divine intent; meritocracy; business interest; nationalistic in military views; anti-government bias; corporations fuel economic growth; unrestricted freedom/choice; law and order/stability; economic wealth defines self and public interest; responsibilities first.	The collective good; private and public interests; religious beliefs private; state to achieve social justice; individual prior to society; economic equality; social intelligence; civil rights.
Related Philosophies	Related Philosophies
Plato-Idealism; Aristotle-Classical Realism; St. Thomas Aquinas, Jacques Barzun-Theistic Realism; William Bagley-Essentialism; Mortimer Adler-Perennialism	John Dewey-Pragmatism; George Counts, William Kilpatrick-Social Reconstructionism

Philosophy gave birth to sociology in the 19th century. Sociologists used the ideas from the Scientific Revolution to focus their efforts on developing adequate scientific theories to explain reality and provide laws of regularities of social events, that is, social facts grounded in empirical knowledge. Four major social theories emerged: (1) a science of society from Functionalism, (2) as science of society from Conflict Theory, (3) a science of human interaction from Symbolic Interactionism, and (4) a science of the individual from Interpretivism.

Science of Society-Functionalism	Science of Society-Conflict Theory	Science of Human Interaction-Symbolic Interactionism	Science of the Individual-Interpretivism
Social institutions seen as analogous to parts of the body; equilibrium of functioning; school as organ of society; individuals chosen for roles and rewarded based on merit; meritocratic society; achieved status; social control.	Social institutions function to preserve inequitable class relations; class domination; capitalists versus workers; mass education to inculcate loyalty to nation/state; reproduction of dominant culture.	The relation of school and society as the development of shared social structure of intelligibility; competence as property of situations; meanings emerge from social interaction.	The individual as interpreter of the world.
Related Ideology Conservatism Related Philosophy Idealism, Realism, Theistic Realism	Related Ideology Marxism Related Philosophy Critical Theory, Postmodernism	Related Ideology Progressive Liberalism Related Philosophy Pragmatism, Progressivism, Social Reconstructionism	Related Ideology Liberalism Related Philosophy Existentialism

Skills to be acquired: I draw from Costa and Kallick (2008) and suggest that class members use a task-specific graphic organizer tool to help them construct knowledge, and organize the ideas from the readings necessary to help them support their arguments. Costa and Kallick (2008) maintain that "These highly structured graphics may seem constraining at times, yet each can be fruitful for students as they systematically approach a task, organize their ideas, and stay focused (especially when the task is complex)" (p. 155).

Class members' reflections at the end of this learning objective are guided by the need to ascertain the degree to which they [1] Adopted a critical eye toward ideas and actions-asked questions to fill in the gap between what was known and what was not known; posed questions about alternative positions or points of view; probed into the causes of

things or just accepted things as they were; posed questions that required a yes or no answer or posed more complex questions [2] Saw things from different perspectives-
changed their mind based on new credible data; approached things in the same way (the
way to which they had become accustomed); perceived things from perspectives other
than their own; or tolerated ambiguity, up to a point [3] Being thoughtful and reflective-
Acted and then thought or thought before acting; strived to clarify and understand what
they heard and read, etc; jumped to offer an opinion about something that they did not
understand fully; considered different possibilities before taking action; accepted the first
idea that came to mind 5] Thinking about own thinking-planned for, reflected on, and
evaluated the quality of their thinking; was increasingly aware of their actions on others;
developed and used mental maps or rehearsed before they performed an action; reflected
on their actions (what they did); wondered about why they were doing what they were
doing; or explained their decision-making process on matters [8] Applying past knowledge to new situations-learned from their experiences; drew on past experience to solve
present problems; approached each new task as though it were the first time; recalled how
they may have solved something in the past that is similar to something on which they are
now working; applied something they learned previously in a new situation [11] Being
cooperative-drew energy from others and sought reciprocity; preferred solitary work; was
sensitive to the needs of others; was a job hog; just wanted to do things only with themselves; let others do all the work for them; was excited about having to justify and test
their ideas on others; was willing to accept feedback from a critical friend [12] Being
attuned and respectful-spoke when others were speaking or did they listen carefully when
others were speaking; paraphrased what they heard others say and accurately expressed
what was said; attended carefully to what others said beneath their words; held in abeyance their judgments and opinions so they could listen to another person's thoughts and
ideas.

   They write their individual reflections in their Habit of Mind Inventory, and, as a
group, reflect on what they learned, and write up those collective reflections in their
Meeting Standards Template. Each learning community shares its work in progress
through Learning Objective 4 with me within one week of the end of the objective.

   A multiple-choice/true/false quiz provides feedback with regard to class members'
retention of key ideas in the readings, while my observations of each group's graphic
organizer serves as my assessment means vis-à-vis class members constructing content
knowledge. To assess group development, I give each class member a Group Performance Scale (using the rubric criteria for judging group performance) and I ask each class
member to rate each of his/her group members.

Learning Objective V

This Learning Objective brings the educational journey to an end, a journey that started in the experience of class participants (they generated their own problem questions, and formulated practical judgments with regard to the problem), moved to class participants acquiring a deeper understanding of the problem through a literature review (examined alternative solutions), continued with class participants offering a working hypothesis (an argument) and their testing that argument logically (a practical judgment to guide action), and now finally concludes with their move to intelligent action, that is, to change (acting on the practical judgment).

Rodgers (2002) suggests that "the movement from experience, to spontaneous interpretation, to naming the problem and reasoning through its complexities must lead to change" (para. 56). The goal in this objective is to help candidates understand that: "One cannot prove that something is valuable by mere argument. Arguments, at best, make certain value judgments plausible as hypotheses-and even then, only if grounded in experience and reflection on the wider consequences of acting on them. Ultimately, the hypotheses must be tested, by seeing how one values the actual results of putting them into practice" (Anderson, 2008, para. 25). The critical goal is to get candidates to test their judgments by acting on them, and to see if they value the consequences to the degree the judgment predicted, that is, be able to confirm or deny the usefulness of the judgment, and, as a result, discover how to live a better life (Anderson, 2008),

Learning Objective V	Content	Skills	Habits of Mind	Assessments for Learning
After being given a working prompt by the instructor, candidates in learning communities will judge how the value judgments in the argument(s) will help to solve the problem in schools today. (evaluate)	Understand that appraisal of value judgments results in new valuing (tool for discovering how to live a better life	Compare and contrast current schooling realities with value judgments in arguments. Use empirical means to assess relevance of value judgments. Group process skills - managerial (mechanisms by which community acts as a unit and not as a loose rabble) and interpersonal (basic manners)	[5] Thinking about own thinking; [8] Applying past knowledge to new situations	Assessment of understanding through oral questioning. Assessment of skills through observations and checklists. Assessment of habits of mind through HoM Inventory and self-assessment.

Content Learning: To get class members to focus on the concept of judgment, I ask them to visualize their driving from home to a class on campus that starts at a specific time. I indicate that they are to imagine that along the way they run into a terrible traffic problem that curtails their movement, and calls into question whether they can get to class on time. My question to the class is "what do you do?" As they share their responses, I help them see that (1) they identified a problem, (2) they were deliberating to find a means to solve the problem posed by the situation (weigh alternatives and their consequences), and (3) they would make a practical judgment. They come to realize that judgment is a complex process of inquiry involving a process of weighing, estimating, testing, facts and hypotheses germane to the solution of a problem.

Practical judgment is instrumental in nature in that the judgment suggests that if X were done then certain consequences Y would follow which would be valued. This form of valuing enables one to test the proposition that is part of the means by which the action is brought about, in other words, decide on a new course of action if necessary.

So, I ask candidates to explain in the first part of the final section of their argumentative papers why others ought to value the judgments they made in their If…then arguments. For example, the learning community should explain why others in education/in the community's particular field ought to pay attention to the community's position on its problem question, and in so doing, get the field to understand that appraisal of value judgments results in new valuing, and is therefore a tool for discovering how to live a better life.

Skills to be acquired: If one wants to uncover new information about the world then the use of a scientific hypothesis is the tool. On the other hand, if one wants to discover how to live a better life then value judgments are the tools. One may test a scientific hypothesis by bringing about antecedents and seeing if the results are as predicted; one may test a value judgment by acting on it and seeing if one values the consequences in the way the judgment predicted. One needs to put the judgment into practice in order to acquire confirming or disconfirming evidence (Anderson, 2008).

So, members of the learning communities must act on their value judgment to see whether they value the consequences in the way the judgment predicted. They must provide evidence of the consequences of acting on the value judgment. In other words, they will be assessing instrumentally how well the value judgments help to solve the problem outlined in the introduction of their argumentative problem inquiry paper. There are three ways by which the foregoing may be done: (1) members of each learning community may describe the results of empirical studies in which the consequences of acting on their value judgments were ascertained; (2) members of each learning community may act on the value judgment in the context of their schools and assess the consequences; or (3) members of each learning community may describe a means of inquiry through which they may test the value judgment. In the latter case, they would need to describe the current realities in their schools [what is] and the changes needed in those schools for their value judgments to work [what ought to be].

Finally, the members of each learning community must describe the changes they will make in their conduct, that is, any revisions in their judgments they have made or will make as a result of the consequences of acting on the value judgments.

Now, at the end of the educational journey, I am able to ask members of each learning community to use the following indicators of good group performance and assess their group's conduct: Members are now eager to be part of the group; individual members feel a sense of autonomy; members are working well together; leadership functions are being shared; and a sense of interdependence has developed.

Candidates also engage in their final reflections on their habits of mind in this learning objective: 5] Thinking about own thinking- they planned for, reflected on, and evaluated the quality of their own thinking; were increasingly aware of their actions on others; developed and used mental maps or rehearsed before they performed an action; reflected on their actions (what they did); wondered about why they did what they did; explained their decision-making process on matters, and [8] Applying past knowledge to new situations-problems (situations); approached each new task as though it were the first time; recalled how they may have solved something in the past that is similar to something on which they are now working; applied something they learned previously in a new situation. They also reflect on their collective learning and its link to standards, and write their reflections in their Meeting Standards Template. Each learning community has a week within which to share the final draft of its argumentative paper with me for my final feedback. Each group is able to make final corrections based on my feedback and then each member of each group uploads a copy of the group's Argumentative Paper and a copy of the group's Meeting Standards Template to the college's electronic Taskstream system.

I provide each class member with a written end of journey course evaluation on his/her performance on (1) the Argumentative Paper and Meeting Standards, (2) Group Performance, and (3) Class Participation.

CHAPTER SIX

GAINING INSIGHT ABOUT ENHANCING HABITS OF MIND FROM CANDIDATES' REFLECTIONS AND SELF-EVALUATIONS

"We reflect on action, thinking back on what we have done in order to discover how our knowing-in-action may have contributed to an unexpected outcome" (Schon, 1983, p. 26).

The purpose in this chapter is to think back on what was done in EDF 6608 Social, Historical and Philosophical Foundations of Education during the summer semester of 2009 in order to discover how my actions and those of the members of the course may have contributed to an unexpected outcome, that is, to new ideas with regard to enhancing reflective intelligence that is practical and professional judgment (capacity to solve pedagogical problems, make informed pedagogical decisions, and generate new knowledge in the world of practice) and the related habits of mind, that is, the disposition toward thinking and acting in the world. Throughout this chapter, candidates' reflections in the course, EDF 6608 Summer A 2009, will be used to ascertain and report candidates' development in their habits of mind, that is in their reflective intelligence.

The class of Summer A, May 4 to June 18, 2009) comprised 25 graduate candidates, 23 females and 2 males. 24 candidates were master's candidates, and 1 was a Ph.D. candidate. The majors of the candidates were as follows: Asian Studies (1), Curriculum and Instruction (2), Early Childhood Education (3), Educational Leadership (5), Exceptional Education (1), Higher Education (7), International/Intercultural Education (2), Music Education (1), TESOL (2), and Urban Education (1).

40% of the class participants indicated that they had never used the WebCT/Blackboard online system. 24% stated that they had used it occasionally, and 36% noted that they used it often. On the other hand, 83% indicated they would be willing to have some of the class sessions online, and 17% were uncertain.

With regard to level of knowledge, 16% had no knowledge of philosophy of education; 52% had limited knowledge; and 32% had somewhat good knowledge. In terms of social theory, 12% had no knowledge; 56% limited knowledge; and 32% somewhat good knowledge. As for history of education knowledge, 12% had no knowledge; 40% limited knowledge; 44% somewhat good knowledge; and 4% very good knowledge.

Interpretive Inquiry

My intent is to make sense of habits of mind by interpreting the meanings members of EDF 6608 had about their experience as provided in their written reflections, my observations, and class documents. This form of intrinsic case study (Stake, 1995) facilitates an analysis of a unique situation. While the central question guiding my interpretive inquiry is "Did the experience in EDF 6608 enhance and nurture reflective intelligence and its related habits of mind?" the intrinsic case study affords me the opportunity to also pursue the following sub-questions: "Did class participants show an inclination and desire to demonstrate habits of mind on the educational journey in EDF 6608? Did the social environment enhance deliberative inquiry? Were the class practices supportive of the habits of mind of reflective intelligence and professional judgment?

That many teacher education candidates bring to the learning experiences in their programs an unreflective propensity has been well documented (Lyutykh, 2009). In fact, Lyutykh (2009) highlights the problem even more so when she describes candidates in her courses this way: "The students often seem detached from the course they take: 'I have to take this course for my certification; tell me what I need to do to get an A, and I want to get over it quickly' (p. 383). Lyutykh (2009) suggests that this attitude may be further reinforced by early schooling socialization, and by the prescriptions of accountability mandates that make getting the right answer the priority (efficiency) instead of candidates having an educative experience (effectiveness). Lyutykh (2009) further notes that when she provides opportunities for her teacher education candidates to engage in thoughtful, reflective activity:

> Without exception, every semester I receive a few e-mails from students asking me to clarify my expectations and meet with them to go over the paper and make sure they did it right....when given such choices...students...treat choice as a lack of organization and 'lack of teaching' on my part....many students reveal their implicit assumption that choosing personal educational experiences upon which to reflect is less important than listening to a PowerPoint presentation and memorizing the definition of *intrinsic motivation*. I believe that this situation is a direct result of educational practices that place more importance on a demonstration of skills than on engagement in critical thinking, thus making the latter a meaningless waste of time (p.p. 382-383).

Some class members in EDF 6608, at the start of the educational journey, did seem to struggle with the need to know immediately what to do, and be given prescriptive details and directions on how to do things. For example, while their feedback about their initial course session revealed their expectations of a mindful learning experience, one also detected some early frustration about not knowing how to complete learning tasks before they even experienced the requisite learning. Some comments at the end of the first class session from which mindful expectations may be extrapolated were:

"This course will teach me how to be more mindful in what I'm learning."

"This evening's experience has given me insight on things I want to focus on that can [make] me a better educator."

"I think this class will be like no other I have taken before. I have been given something to learn instead of a task to do and learn through it."

"It seems like an interesting and challenging experience."

"It is not always about book knowledge but about personal experience."

"We will be having a lot of discussions and shared experiences in this class. We will pose questions, address issues, and use valid arguments to prove our points of interest."

"I am glad this is a class where I can learn through my experiences instead of test taking."

"I expect that this course will bring forth analytical skills that I have never fully developed."

"You (Erskine) have given me a perfect first impression of what I am getting into. I am very excited to see what is to come."

"There are no clear answers only more questions."

"It seems that being in this course I will experience a new way of learning."

"I am greatly relieved that this course is based on using and becoming and not just this guy said this 200 years ago. The foundations class I completed as an undergraduate was pure memorization of names and theory; no application."

"Now I understand why we do not need textbooks."

On the other hand, candidates' initial feedback and excerpts from their Habits of Mind Inventory reveal the urge for routine, and approaching things in the manner to which they had become accustomed:

"Somewhat more open, loose – don't know how comfortable that makes me."

"No midterm/final which I was expecting,"

"This should be a growth experience. I'm surprised by the no mid-term/final."

"My first day of class (I could not attend the first day) was very confusing. I had read the professor's emails and it contained terms foreign to me. The syllabus was called a "map". I've used maps before. I have a GPS now, so a map seems archaic in these times, but maps have been useful to me in the past. I used on my way from Gainesville to Jacksonville in college. There was a clear distinction between that map and our "map". The map I used to get to Jacksonville had a clear beginning and end for me. I started in one place and ended in another. But, where is our "map" taking us? What kind of "journey" is the professor talking about? I was lost before I even looked closely at the map. I prejudged this journey before I got a full understanding of it. Allowing the professor to explain his reasoning and withhold judgment was is a key indicator that I am starting to the thoughtful in actions."

"This course began differently than most others. Instead of diving right into the content and discussing when we would have our first test, we discovered that there would be no exams and spent most of the first night analyzing a metaphor of an "educational journey" and jumping on the bus. When it was revealed that the journey needed a map that was the syllabus I calmed down a little. I am very familiar with syllabi and they always provide a nice reference point when I am confused. Then I discovered that the syllabus for this class was very long and I felt less comforted."

"I see that Erskine keeps telling us to slow down and understand the journey. That our groups must all be on the bus and able to communicate and listen to what each of us has to offer. That our Syllabus is our map but not the Journey. That the Journey is our experiences along the way. Erskine wants us to be open minded and that we have to be willing to let other people help guide us along our journey. We should be able to communicate amongst each other and come up with new ideas and information. All this is great and I agree with it 100%. But I am not sold on this idea. Because, I am not able to put a connection to how we are supposed to write our paper. I feel like I don't have the knowledge of our actual argument. We can discuss our views and opinions all we want but we really don't have a full understanding on our topic. I don't feel that I am being closed minded. I am trying to understand Erskine's way of teaching but I'm just not getting it. Maybe because I am not used to this approach of teaching."

"On a normal basis I usually always have the same routine of looking up courses, making sure the professor had good ratings, going to class constantly and making sure I listen and get the work done for the semester. Someone asked me how my first day of class went and all I said was that it was "enlightening." I did not really grasp the whole idea at first; I was at awe at what was being said and the assignments that would be considered. However, Erskine did a wonderful job of making the connections in the syllabus with the whole idea of what our class was initially going to be about. I actually was excited to go on this journey. I knew it was going to be worthwhile. Did I question the timing and the work that needed to be completed, yes I did, but Erskine knew exactly how to ease everyone's worries. I communicated with my community further about questions and comments in regards to our problem question and knew that I was going to gain a whole lot more than just a few credits."

"On the first day of class I found myself trying to make sense of the "educational journey" our professor kept speaking about. He then completely lost me when he mentioned that we would not be taking a midterm exam or a final exam. I pondered as to how he was going to base our final grade since every other course I had previously taken the professors had based their grades on their student's exam grades. I noticed that my mind was working a mile a minute trying to figure out answers to questions that hadn't been asked."

"One of the difficulties I am having in class is trying to jump ahead without understanding the basis/process. I find myself having to slow down in order to understand the purpose. I guess it's kind of like Piaget's stages of development, which looks at introducing new concepts – when the mind is ready. In other words, early exposure to a concept does not help students, if their mind is not at that level yet. Despite all of my feelings, I discovered in each class session that by slowing down – I actually learn more. I also get to see and understand the bigger picture, instead of feeling lost in the smaller things. If you understand the foundation – the rest comes easier. After all, like my mother always says – you can't start building a house from the top down. She is a very wise woman you know."

"I really did not know where and how to begin writing my own the Habits of Mind. I was nervous about completing it the wrong because when it comes to school I do tend to concentrate on the end result. The fact of the matter is that school is designed with the end in mind and grades are a part of how schools run so to completely ignore that I feel would be foolish. In other aspects of my life I have a laissez faire attitude but not in class and I think I have to adjust to the new notions set by Erskine. I found myself questioning Erskine's methods."

Lyutykh (2009) found the following contradiction in her classes:

The college of education where I teach requires instructors to use a rubric to assess students' CT [critical thinking] dispositions. According to the rubric, students' written work and class participation must demonstrate that they are curious, receptive to new ideas or multiple perspectives, and appreciative of the course content as relevant to their future teaching endeavors. However, the students often exhibit beliefs that are inconsistent with the official definition of this disposition (383).

I also noted a discrepancy in some of the candidates in EDF 6608 between their initial self-ratings on the habits of mind, and their initial conduct in the course. For example, the initial top five ratings for the twelve habits of mind (a 1-5 point rating scale-5 being does consistently, and 1 does very little) by class members were 1. Being Open-minded (4.33) 2. Think about own Thinking (4.33), 3 and 4 Transfer Learning to New Situation and Care for Others and Listen Well (4.29), and 5. Act on the basis of own Initiative (4.13). However, my initial observations of class members' conduct revealed that (1) many class members found the course operation as different from what they were accustomed to, and were exhibiting frustrating behaviors and not open-mindedness, (2) many class members had initial difficulty writing a reflection of their learning experience, an inability to think about their own thinking (3) many class members were not transferring what was done at one step to the next, (4) some class members spoke when another class member was speaking, and there was little paraphrasing of what others said, and (5) many class members were attributing their not understanding something immediately to failure and not to growth possibility, and they seem to be driven more by the need to get the right answer (the teacher's answer) and less by the process to find the answer.

Course Experience and Growth in Habits of Mind

So, did the experience in EDF 6608 enhance and nurture reflective intelligence and its related habits of mind? What happened on and during the educational journey that may have enhanced growth in the habits of mind? An examination of course members' reflective entries in their Habits of Mind Inventory provide the following insights.

Reflections in Habits of Mind Inventory about Being Thoughtful

Candidates recognized the need to manage impulsivity:

"I learned not to jump to conclusions. I discovered this during the online discussions. You need to hear out all the details before you express your thoughts right off the bat."

"As the professor was explaining Plato and I realized that his philosophy was different than what I thought, I had the urge to just stop reading it. I was once again acting without thinking. It took me a while to think that just because Plato's philosophy was not what I expected it does not mean that I will not read it. I decided after careful thought that I will read Plato's Republic as soon as I get a chance. Therefore, I went ahead and bought the book."

"One of the difficulties I am having in class is trying to jump ahead without understanding the basis/process. I find myself having to slow down in order to understand the purpose. I guess it's kind of like Piaget's stages of development, which looks at introducing new concepts—when the mind is ready. In other words, early exposure to a concept does not help students, if their mind is not at that level yet. Despite all of my feelings, I discovered in each class session that by slowing down – I actually learn more. I also get to see and understand the bigger picture, instead of feeling lost in the smaller things. If you understand the foundation—the rest comes easier. After all, like my mother always says— you can't start building a house from the top down. She is a very wise woman you know."

They learned to work to understand before offering an opinion, and to think before acting:

"During this most enlightening part of our course, I found myself thinking before acting. For example during our discussion about Plato, I first tried to understand his philosophy and then judge it from my point of view and decided not to agree with it. This serves as an example of how I tried to clarify what I heard and read during our discussions. I did not jump to offer an opinion about something I did not understood. On the contrary, if I did not understand something, I asked to make clarifications. I found myself considering different possibilities before taking action. Instead of accepting the first idea that came to my mind, I decided to think about other possibilities and accept the best option."

"My first day of class (I could not attend the first day) was very confusing. I had read the professor's emails and it contained terms foreign to me. The syllabus was called a "map". I've used maps before. I have a GPS now, so a map seems archaic in these times, but maps have been useful to me in the past. I used on my way from Gainesville to Jacksonville in college. There was a clear distinction between that map and our "map". The map I used to get to Jacksonville had a clear beginning and end for me. I started and one place and ended in another. But, where is our "map" taking us? What kind of "journey" is the professor talking about? I was lost before I even looked closely at the map. I prejudged

\this journey before I got a full understanding of it. Allowing the professor to explain his reasoning and withhold judgment was is a key indicator that I am starting to the thoughtful in actions."

"I am striving to manage my impulsivity and think before I speak. In my learning community, I considered different possibilities in our philosophical questions before taking action. One of our group members really liked my original idea, but instead of jumping to begin with that thought, we continued exploring until we decided on our questions by comparing it to different possibilities. I was careful not to act rashly and decide for the group what our philosophical problem statement would be, but rather bounce ideas back and forth and clarify any misunderstandings on our ideas. Before finally choosing the question, we considered three possibilities: "1) Should students be grouped homogeneously based on sex or heterogeneously based in the principles of democracy, 2) "Should foreign language students be tested on the FCAT math and science in their native languages", or 3) "Should public schools with a certain percentage of LEP students offer bilingual programs"? After consulting with the professor, we chose our question, but not after wrestling with all possibilities."

"This habit of mind is the most relatable (in my opinion) and the most exercised in this learning objective. At the beginning of our discussions, I was extremely quick to answer any question without necessarily thinking it through. I am not usually like this, as my mom always told me to 'connect my brain to my tongue,' and I am usually quiet not because I have nothing to say, but I am thinking about what to say, how to say what I am thinking, and when. Because of my past experiences with online discussions, I knew that in order to get your two cents in, you had to type as quickly as possible and put in your answer soon after the question was posed. How absolutely wrong was I. The professor tried very hard to make us think about our responses before writing the first thing that came to mind and calling certain groups to make certain everything was clarified for everyone. No other guided instruction of any other habit of mind has been shown so clearly. When I hear that instructors are responsible for developing habits of mind, I don't quite believe it. How can instructors be responsible for forming habits? This seems like a simple answer: 'of course they are'! But thinking realistically, how can any education programs really teach you how to do that? I've never seen a Miami-Dade professional development geared toward that. I didn't get my bachelors in education so maybe my perceptions of Schools of Education are skewed. However, during the discussions I saw an example of how an educator can be a facilitator for the teaching of habits. This information is invaluable to me because I teach at a leadership magnet school that follows Covey's Seven Habits of Highly Effective People and adapts them to middle school children. It occurred to me that I probably knew how to teach habits, I just never thought of it as anything out of the ordinary. Thanks to Dr. Dottin's guidance, I was able to think about questions before answering them and striving for clarity whenever possible."

"I had to go and visit the professor in order to get some clarification because I didn't want to start or continue with our argumentative paper without fully comprehending what was expected from the group."

Candidates' reflections show evidence of their working to consider different possibilities before taking action:

"Before I started to write to this reflection, I never thought about the fact that I might make a decision before looking at different possibilities. Yet, it has happened so many times that by just being able to see it now, I realize that it has to stop. Now, I see that some of the mistakes I have made in my life are due to the fact that I have participated in a decision without looking at all the options first. For example, I always thought that the habits of mind inventory had only one entry per objective. It was not until the professor wrote back to me to tell me that I needed to do the other objectives that I realized that it was more complex. I failed to look at all the other possibilities; I accepted the first idea that came to mind, 'one entry per objective.' I did not take the time to look further and check if I completed all the assignment. It is amazing how little things in life teach you so much. After today, I will always scroll down to see if there are more habits of mind within one objective."

Reflections in Habits of Mind Inventory about Persisting

Entries in the Habits of Mind Inventory showed that candidates did not always succumb to the temptation to give up when answers were not immediately known, but worked to see things through:

"During learning objective 1 I really wanted to give up. Not just because of the assignment. it was the accumulation of this and my other two classes and my group morale. I guess there was a problem with the pre-quiz and everyone was not in great spirits. The solution was not immediately apparent but I do want to stick to the task. A problem we are having is that there is not much peer reviewed information or research on our topic and we were getting frustrated in our research efforts. By the end of the night, I think we were demonstrating this habit as we all went home and continued working together as a group online."
"I learned that patience is key! You cannot think you will have one thing done right away. The literature review showed me this. It takes time to organize all your research and synthesize the information."

Candidates recognized that setting up a system helps one to persist in completing tasks:

"A good way for me to complete a task is to write down everything that I want to accomplish and get that done. Once that is completed I will be able to move on to something else. As for doing the research for our topic, it does get frustrating when you can't find something that you are looking for. But I try not to be a quitter. I do understand that when I start to get frustrated it is best to stop what I'm doing, relax and then come back to it. And that's what I did when I wasn't getting the results I wanted. One thing that really helped me find quality information was to use the Boolean style or research. By changing the words and also using the synonyms I was able to find the information I wanted easier."

"On Monday night we stayed late to finish our introduction to make sure that we were able to complete it to turn it in on Wednesday. We jotted down a large number of ideas and on Tuesday and Wednesday we spoke back and forth on e-mail and by phone to make correction to the introduction and objective standards to turn it in to the professor so that we could get feedback from him. Even though this was such a long process we felt it was important to create a good product rather than to finish it quickly. We really agonized with the ideas we came up to formulate a working introduction for our argumentative paper."

"I found myself wanting to stick to the group paper until it was completed. Even though it is not easy to get everyone in the same page, I wanted to make sure that we all had the same goals in producing a good, high quality argumentative paper. I didn't find myself giving up on things that I didn't know, however I did find myself being distracted by questions that kept coming up. It's funny because I did find myself coming up with a systematic system to guide us in our paper. I suggested that we would divide the work in equal portions and that we would all read what we wrote and give ourselves feedback. I also saw myself agreeing with one of my group members that the best way to meet, it seemed was through e-mail."

"This journey has not been an easy one. I have found myself plenty of times being uninterested in writing my reflections. At times it felt as if they were a waste of time and that more focus should have been put on composing the argumentative paper. It seems as though once you finish one task you have two others already lined up with the third in tow. For many students, working a full-time job and taking a graduate course can be stressful. Both demand deadlines and one cannot really pick and chose which to complete first as they both have the same importance. In speaking to my group mates we came to realize that we hadn't really worked on a system to try to get things accomplished. We then decided to meet after each class meeting to complete the work that was due the following class meeting. This was able to help in the beginning of class but once the ball began to roll we realized that more time needed to be spent together to work on our assignments. Since then we have set up group meetings throughout the week as well as weekends. With the overwhelming amount of work that is required for this class I don't think we really have had time to be distracted. It seems that we are working like robots and follow a daily pattern that equal work-school-school work."

Reflections in Habits of Mind Inventory about Being Cooperative

Candidates worked with and learned from others in reciprocal situations:

"Our group went from forming to performing fairly quickly. The storming period was extremely brief-and I don't think I would even consider that 'storming'-just a time where we were exploring different ideas and maybe disagreed on where our passions were. I felt like a job hog when I came up with some ideas on my own to share with the group, but I really did that to be able to share rather than spend time in class coming up with ideas and then sharing-something that would have wasted some time. While doing group work, there is a time where some independent things must be done in order to benefit the speed and efficiency of the whole group."

"After learning about the works of Plato and Dewey, our group met twice to discuss our thoughts on the readings and draw ideas from each other. At this point, it is not a good idea to be a job hog because we are all on the same boat- we have to connect our ideas to the readings for the betterment of our paper. This was the most important time to get together and synergize- act like a real group- rather than work alone."

"Although, I have always preferred to work by myself because I have had a lot of bad experiences working in groups, I am glad that this course allows me to work with other people. This course has a very complicated nature of the course because it defies the natural order of things. For example, the idea of backward learning is not used every day and in every course. I feel that if I would have had to formulate a question by myself, it would have been much harder than doing it in groups. I also like the fact that the professor put us together based on majors. It allowed us to have similar ideas. For example, two group members had very good ideas that were not dramatically different from mine. We ended up choosing one out of three that each of us formulated, after we talked about them. If I would have done this by myself, I probably would not have been able to formulate the question is such a short period of time. It would have taking me longer and I would not have been able to meet my deadline."

"It has been a long time since I have done actually group work in a collegiate course. Most of the time, especially after beginning the masters program when a group assignment was given by a professor we generally split the work up and go on our merry way. Every person in responsible for their own part but there was no discussion as to what each group member was doing or any discussion about the topic at hand. So far the experience in Erskine's class has been so different. As a group we are all collaborating to come up with one cohesive finished product. As we tossed ideas out we began to formulate what would be our introduction. In the past one person would complete the introduction and turn it in for the group and as the project progressed others would complete different parts of the project, but in this instance we are all building one artifact together. I like this process better because it allows us to build on the notion that our ideas are not the only ones that need to be listened to."

"Comparing this course with the previous one I had taken, I was kind of nervous when I heard that we would be assigned into groups. I had only taken one graduate course prior to this one and it required individual work which consisted of writing a research paper. The uneasiness stemmed from the horror stories that I had heard from friends and colleagues about being forced to work in groups. They all complained about having a group member who did not like to participate but was willing to complain when they were being reprimanded about their lack of participation. So far, I have had no issues with my group members and very pleased with the selection the professor made when teaming me up with other individuals. We all come from different backgrounds of education which made it easier for us to jot down ideas of our topic. We were able to give constructive criticism on our ideas such as whether they made sense and flowed well enough to put in our paper. Our professor provided us with feedback on how our group was coming along in the developmental stages. He labeled us as being in the "norming and moving to performing" stage. Stemming from his feedback it seems that we are on the right track! We now have a good sense of security within ourselves. From this we can strive to work harder in generating a well prepared argumentative paper."

"Whenever I hear the words "group work", I tremble. Some experiences related to team work have not always been so pleasant. Usually one or two people carry the load for the whole team – then every one gets the same grade. Talk about fairness, a term we discussed in class today. I was quite tense when I heard that we were writing an argumentative paper within our group. However, this experience, thus far has been great! I love the idea of having a new leader each week. This way everyone gets an equal chance to lead. The group evaluation sheet that we fill out at the end of each session is very helpful; as it helps the group members to stay focused on a goal."

They drew energy from others:

"The professor shared forming, norming, storming and performing stages which a group goes through. The forming stage already makes sense to me. We want to perform as a group. We all contributed to our group's development in a manner that helps the group reach the performing stage, the evidence of which should be a well developed argumentative paper."

"The reason I mentioned in one of my previous reflections that our group have been able to run smoothly is because we all came up with different ideas and we all contributed to the final question. For example, one member and I wrote the pro and cons of the argument, another member on the other hand, wrote about the democratic principles and searched for articles that supported our point of view."

"Although I have chosen to work alone in the past I was excited by the opportunity to function as a group. I felt it would be a learning experience and might even be fun. My worry was that we would be distracted and have trouble focusing on our topic. It turns out, since we all had common goals and busy schedules we were determined to work together effectively. When things were confusing me about what topics to research I found that discussing them after the research lecture was the best way to relieve my confusion. It was great to bounce ideas off of each other. I found myself drawing energy and motivation from the other girls in my group and I did my best to provide it for them. I found myself being sensitive to the needs of others. One member works in the after school care program and I was careful to be mindful of this when discussing times for future meetings. We agreed as a group to split the key concepts of the lit review. It was great to share the work load and provide and receive feedback."

"As a group the first thing we did was divide up our readings that way we each can take a section and focus on that section. We did this because of the amount of time we have to get everything done. We wanted to be as productive as we can. Not to rush and try to get it done as fast as we could but to allow us to have the time to fully understand what we are reading and what we need to accomplish."

"When Erskine asked us to come up with one reason to support our topic we began generating a series of ideas as a group. All of us listened to each other, and I was asked by my group members to take the lead during that class session

I drew so much energy from our in class session on Dewey and Plato. I really tired to understand what everyone was saying because I did not want to speak without offering anything constructive to the class discussion. When one member tried to pose a question on Plato as a group we are so in tune with each other that I felt her getting frustrated before she actually got frustrated. I interjected in the conversation to try and clarify what she was saying because I wanted her voice to be heard rather than my own, and also to show her support by letting her know that I understood what she was saying. Our whole group actually did the same thing which shows that we draw from each others energy to show support for one another and to try to understand the topics being discussed. I mean instead of meeting individually in our houses to chat we prefer to meet in one spot and chat together, sometimes using the same computer when we are having technical difficulties. We rather learn together than apart."

"At the beginning I was a little bit worried about a project with a group, but as we discussed "what ought to be" problems, I was deeply impressed with my group members' knowledge and enthusiasm. As we progress, I started to like group activities and sharing community. We see each other on Saturdays and call when we have troubles. I am feeling comfortable now. Only worry I have is we might depend on one member who is the coordinator for the paper a lot. But she is very proud of her position, and may be it is fair for her though she is busier than us. If I were fluent in English, I would love to be a coordinator; therefore I should respect her position and rely on her. This depending on somebody is a new task for me. Because in Japan, when I was working as an executive at the company, I was the one to whom other workers followed. Now I am learning not only academically but also how to be humble yet productive and creative member in a sharing community, and surprisingly, I love it!! Before I started our journey, I was not sure about group work, but I have come to realize that I can learn a lot from my group members. Since I did not know any educational system of the U.S., they gave me information and really helped me to write literature review. I am glad that I could help them with my knowledge of writing references. I felt good that I am contributing at some part."

"I usually enjoy working by myself, and I expressed some apprehension at the beginning of this journey about working in groups, especially one with five members and all women. The way we've been able to work together, to share responsibilities, and to trust each other with each part of the project, and ultimately our grade in the class, still amazes me. I'm truly blessed to be in such great company. We're even planning to celebrate our four-week anniversary next week. Silly, I know, but I love the message that it conveys. We care about each other and respect each other very much."

"This group activity has been one of the most rewarding things I've ever done, and I want to thank you, Dr. Dottin, for the opportunity. I've gotten to know these three amazing women (the fourth one was already a close friend) who before were just classmates. As I've mentioned before, from day one we were able to agree on how to do things, and there hasn't been any animosity among us. We support each other when one doesn't understand or can't finish a section. We adapt to each other's needs and have been able up to this point to complete each assignment without arguing. On the contrary, I'm sure you and the rest of the class have witnessed what great energy and dynamics we experience when we get together."

They were sensitive to the needs of others:

"It was very comforting at the beginning when set up with my group members to know each one was in the same program as me. I definitely found myself sensing the energy of the others and enjoying group with them. I definitely found myself being considerate of the feelings of others and wanting to make sure everyone's voice was heard and everyone participated equally. I definitely made it a point to request critical feedback from each member. I found it was not a difficult task as a group to create our introduction."

"As I mentioned in one of my previous habits of minds, I have always preferred to work alone rather than in groups. However, in this course I am part of an excellent group. We all know our responsibilities and we respect each other's points of view. In addition, we are able to divide the work equally and we don't mind going a step ahead to help each other. I feel that we are all here to help each other and I am very sensitive to my group's need. If I need to go the extra mile to help other members with their research or anything else, I will."

"With my section I had to read it about three or four times to fully understand it. I also couldn't read it that many times in one day. I had to put it down and think about what I read. I would then pick it up again and read it over. I also highlighted and took notes on my readings. That way I can compare my thoughts from one day to the next. This also made it easier to explain to my group members."

"As I previously mentioned, our team is very supportive and understanding. When I was getting frustrated with the literature review, the rest of the team members were very helpful and encouraged me to keep searching. Some even said that they would search on their own and send me any pertinent article they could find. As I was searching, I came across articles that pertained to some of the group members, and so I immediately emailed them to them."

"As I've mentioned before, this project has been challenging for me, but I've had no problem asking my teammates for clarification when there's an idea I don't understand. When one finds a link between the readings and our argument, she readily shares it with the rest. Some of us have even gone as far as volunteering to complete parts of the assignment that could've easily been split among a few members simply because she had the time and felt like helping the rest out."

They were excited about having to justify and test their ideas on others:

"Once we all had read and understood each of our sections we then got together as a group and spoke about what we each had learned. Even though we had our own separate readings we were still able to grasp the whole concept of the chapters because we shared our thoughts and ideas on Dewey as well as ourselves. Through our discussions we were able to talk about our argument and start to put the pieces together."

"Through constant communication our group was really getting the hang of things. Each time we understood something it was definitely a good feeling. We were able to understand our problem questions and how it relates to Dewey. This also helped us put together our thoughts and ideas to start to write our arguments."

"During the library session I saw myself preferring to work alone. I knew that everyone was at different points in their graduate careers and I felt that I was going to be slowed down if I had to explain how to do a literature review. However, when talking to my group members, I realized that they all had different experiences and even thought they might not have been too familiar with doing a literature review, they brought other skills to the table. I was able to hear what they had to say about our argument and I became more open-minded with what they had to say and offer."

"I don't want to be a hog for this assignment. Thank god we are doing this as a group. I'm also thankful about the way we've been able to split this assignment into parts, how each member just pull her way, and how great we work together. Our professor gave us suggestions to guide us along with the support for our argumentative paper. He understands that we have several obstacles against us: time and lack of knowledge of philosophy. Before the end of Wednesday's class, our team had already discussed who was going to read which chapter. One person gives suggestions, and we all agree as if by magic. I can't wait to read my section and find out how I'll help my team with the support needed for our paper. It's going to be challenging but also rewarding."

They were willing to accept feedback:

"I like to work in groups because I feel it gives you a better understanding on the overall goal. I feel that by discussing our argument we can get different perspectives. One thing that draws me from group projects is the fact that we all have different schedules and that it might not be the most convenient time to meet. But we have to work as a team and we all need to give and take in order to have the best results. At times I feel like it is easier to just take the work upon myself just to get it done the right way faster. Although, in situations like this I am glad we are working in a group. (I'm hoping we all can lean on each other.) When we are able to express our frustrations to each other and you get feedback from the other group members, it makes me feel like I'm not doing this alone and that there are others in my same situation who can help me understand the problems better."

"When it came to doing research we felt that the best way to gather information was to do so on our own time. This way it was allowing each of us to use our minds and references to come up with different sources. By doing this we were able to find different articles to help us write our paper. We also decided that once we have found our research we were going to write a little about what we had found. This way when we meet up again we were able to get the ball rolling. We each shared what we had written. We talked about the pros and cons of our finds and made sure that we took the best parts of what we found. This was a way to get great feedback and make sure that we were all on the right page. We then started to put the pieces together to create out literature review."

Reflections in Habits of Mind Inventory that Highlight the Importance of Reflection

"The best thing about this class is the reflection part. It really makes you think about what you are thinking, which gave me a better understanding of what the journey was about. Reflection is key!"

"The above features that I have learned about myself can help me become a better teacher. I know that I need to constantly reflect on what I do. I can not act on impulse, I have to be patient and get a full understanding of the situation. I know that feedback is key for my students. I need to let them know what they could do to make things better or what they did that was great."

"I learned that there are qualities that a person may think he has, but will not know for sure until he puts them to the test. I learned that practice makes perfect, and that to acquire, maintain and develop good qualities takes conscious effort and practice, as well as continues renewal. This is accomplished through constant reflection. A famous mathematician once said 'the unexamined life is not worth living,' I think I have a deeper understanding now what he meant. I learned that I'm a lot more capable than I thought I was. To be honest before this class I was doing well academically, but as a person I had become stagnant. I knew I could become better, I just didn't know how."

"I have learned that my capacity for learning extends much more than I envisioned once I started this course. Although, I have always been a good student and enjoyed education I did not believe I could actually be scholarly material. This belief was founded by my lower SAT and GRE scores than my native born colleagues. I have learned throughout that it has been my perseverance all along that has allowed me to experience the fruits of education. For the first time, I really experience a connection with what I am learning in the classroom and my work at the college. I have always been a person to do much reflection but it has been usually in my mind. This time my reflections are much more meaningful because once they take a written form you own them and want to share your enlightenment with others. I specially want to share my enthusiasm with my son and daughter who both are teenagers and will be starting college soon. I want to inspire them to continue their education actively. I am eager to share with my colleagues at the college and my students as well. I like to share with family and friends as well but it is not always easy for them to understand the value of learning because they are tying to the means of a particular job and salary."

Reflections in Habits of Mind Inventory that Highlight Things Learned about Self

Adopting a critical eye

"I can definitely say I grew when it came to thinking more critically. I was used to all of my past courses following the same old routine and the structure of this course definitely provided me with a different viewpoint of learning."

Being Open-minded

"This semester I learned that I was not as opened minded as I thought. It's not that I'm closed minded, but it takes me a little longer to get accustomed to new situation. I saw myself becoming frustrated when new things were introduced to me. It wasn't the material that was being taught to me, but the way the class was structured. There were many

things that were going on in my personal life this semester and I believe that had to do
something with me not truly comprehending what the professor wanted us to get out of
this class. I guess what I really learned about myself is that I need to be able to separate
things and leave your troubles at home. I discovered that it is really hard for me to concentrate on school material when family problems arise."

Working to See Things Through

"This course which was a journey allowed me to learn to never give up and the importance of persistence and pushing oneself and others in a group to get a task complete! I
learned to be more open minded when I initially do not understand something. In addition
I learned everyone has a different system of doing things so it's important to be very patient and understanding. Also this course reinforced the importance of communication."
"I am learning a lot about myself and the main thing is that I need limit and discipline to
get into the rhythm required for studying. I am very friendly but this is also a bad thing
because I don't like confrontations and then I postpone important decisions to avoid conflict."
"I also learned that I work under pressure, so sometimes I postpone things and on the last
minute I get it done, but this is not always good, because sometimes I find myself with
lack of time to complete the activities."
"This journey has opened my eyes a little more on what I learned about myself. I know
that I am a hard working person that can work diligently with other members in a group. I
learned that I can focus on very important tasks in a very small amount of time. I know
now that no task is too hard for me. I learned that reflecting and feedback are very important concepts that I can use in the future to better myself as an educator."

Thinking Interdependently

"I learned that I still don't like writing long reflection pieces or working in groups because although I try very hard to be accommodating, I like to micro-manage anything that
has to do with school or assignments. I don't like to rely on other people for things that
affect my future, although now that I think about it, we do everyday. I rely on doctors to
treat me, I rely on police officers to help me and so on. I think what I don't like is relying
on others in instances where I control my own fate. Could I learn to control this and do
group work anyway? Of course I can. In life one must learn to do things we don't always
want to do. On the upside, I did learn that I can make the best out of a situation where I
don't necessarily feel like I can do my best work."
"In this class I learned that working in groups is an experience that I appreciate, especially if the group is as cohesive as the one we formed with SpectruMagic. One of my
teammates mentioned last night during our last class session that this is the first time that
she's experienced both hard work and so much fun while in a group. We really did have
an awesome time together. I learned that I could be much more patient than I thought
and that I could learn to work with others and relinquish control when trust is present. I
also learned to slow down and make connections through reflections."

"I learned that I can actually enjoy working in a group. Before this class I was forced to work in groups and usually I just did my section of the work, the day before the class we would meet and stick our product together, and never really learn from each other. The way the argumentative paper was structured we had to learn to be interdependent. We had to rely on each other to be able to send Erskine a decent finished product. I realized that sometimes completing tasks together makes for a good learning experience."

"I learned that being dependent is not a bad thing. Society makes a person believe that if an individual is dependent on another then that signifies the person to being weak in their abilities. In my current job title my duties require for me to work alone, so I've always been used to getting things done on my time and not really needing or seeking assistance from others but after this class it taught me that without relying on others our work would not have gotten done. I learned to be interdependent, to be able to work in a group with having others contributing in order to complete a collective task. I also learned that reflection assist in progression. If you are able to make connections with the content that you learned you are able to excel in the material. You are then more knowledgeable in the topic because you are able to apply it to different scenarios/occasions. I learned by observing other groups that not everyone is able to work together if there is a lack of open-mindedness. When you keep an open mind, things or situations are better understood."

"I learned that my role in the group was similar to my role in my family, that of a mediator. When one group member was upset and distant I would call to assure them that we were on the right track. I think I learned in this class without actually noticing (focusing) in only that. I learned that you can teach an old dog (me), new tricks. A literature review would have been a scary thing, if I would have had to approach it alone. I discovered that live chatting is not as bad as I thought it would be. At times it was too fast and the feedback was not provided, but we learned none the less from the transcripts of the lesson."

"Throughout this journey I learned that working in a group with strangers is not as hard as it seems as long as every group member is willing to cooperate with each other. I also learned that to justify an argument, facts are not always necessary. One could also use philosophical ideas."

"I learned that I am a natural leader. Even when it wasn't my turn to "lead" the group I still found myself initiating discussions and checking with all group members for understanding or need to clarification. I also learned that working in a group is not as terrible as I thought it might be."

Acting on the Basis of Own Initiative

"I learned that I am more prone to be stressed out when I feel that I have limited choices. I learned that I can be shy. This was the first time that I have ever questioned my academic ability. I hesitated on asking questions because I was afraid of being judged. I also learned that I learn better in environments that are conducive to dialectic methods. I like this course because I was involved in it; in oppose to just taking it. I felt like an active participant. Although, at times I wanted to jump ship and drop the course."

Being Thoughtful

"My initial impression of this course was frustration. In learning more about what and how we are learning, I now understand that I was trying to absorb things without understanding them or why they were important....I enjoy being insightful but struggle with not getting immediate gratification in mastery of my understanding."

"One of the things that I learned in this journey about myself was that I needed to look in depth into an argument. Even, if I don't agree with it. The key is to understand what the author is trying to portray. I also learned that I need to try different ways to approach an argument. For example, if I do not understand what Dewey means by Dualism, I should go back and re-read the definition of it or try to identify its meaning in context. I also learned the importance of getting along with your group members. I realized that the best way to get along is to communicate with your group members and express what you think. I also realized that I am more flexible than what I thought."

"The biggest thing that I learn was to be patient. In the past as well as now I try my very best to take one day at a time. With this class I didn't do that in the beginning. I had to constantly remind myself to slow down and get on the bus, don't try to solve everything in the beginning. At least that is what Erskine was telling us. But of course I wanted to get it all in the first day of class. But for this class if you don't take it one day at a time then you will get frustrated and feel like you are falling behind. I soon realized that that wasn't the case. Looking back at all those times I was frustrated and felt like I was dumb were all just a waist of energy. I realized that it is okay to not understand the first time, that if I can at least start to write something down and reflect upon what I wrote then I will understand it a little more each time, and that's exactly what I did. I made sure to ask many questions and constantly try improve. I realized that we are in groups to learn about ourselves as well as others, and I learned how reflect upon what others do and say."

Caring and Listening

"Learning Objective #4-This was my favorite learning objective as it pertains to this habit of mind. I say favorite not because I feel I exhibit the habit of mind better than the others, but because this is when I most noticed how much people (myself included) needed to learn to exhibit this habit of mind better. In the online sessions, it seemed everyone wanted to say their piece and repeated the same things over and over just to be heard (or in the case of online learning-seen.) I noticed the same thing occurred whether we were learning online or whether we were in the classroom. I think this habit of not listening carefully, paraphrasing what others say and not listening actively stems from participation grades. In K-12 schools, participation is an important aspect of a grade. However, if a teacher doesn't remember that you contributed, your grade will eventually suffer. This makes students *overly* participate at the expense of others. When those shy students realize their grades are suffering, they start to speak on top of others and that creates chaos. I think we experienced some of that in our discussions. It was a good way of showing though, how this habit of mind is extremely difficult to develop and sustain."

"In the first couple of weeks, I would try to dominate any discussion in the group, however, I do have manners and I would never speak over anyone, I would listen, but generally my mind was already made up as to what course of action I would like to take, in other words, I was not being open minded. I became a better listener after the second online chat, the one we had on Plato that is when I finally realized that you first need to fully understand the idea before making a judgment. I also realize that you need to think about the different perspective and how it apply to the overall picture or in our case the problem question in our argumentative paper. As the weeks progressed I became a much better listener, I could interpret exactly what the people in my group were trying to convey. It was as if a hearing aid had been inserted in my brain. I realized toward the end that I was no longer wanted to impose my idea if it was not the best one. In other words if someone in my group came up with something that made more sense I would go with it. I think I have definitely become more open minded, I became more interested in the collective good, than in my individual self interest."

Transfer of Habits of Mind

So, will the capacity for judgment learned in the course show up later on the job? Based on candidates' reflective entries, the following capacities were activated and set in motion.

Instructional Transfer

"After this learning experience, I hope to continue exercising good habits of mind. At the beginning of the new school year, I plan on engaging my students to reshape their way of thinking and of looking at grades. Hopefully I can make an impact by facilitating their learning and thinking experience."

"Using the example of my students and making connections without being explicitly told what to do, I feel that if I make an attempt to consciously apply the habits of mind into my lesson plans, I can not only practice them myself, but become a true educator- one that not only wants to impart knowledge on a certain subject or material, but one that wants to educate and develop the student as a whole."

"One of my main goals to becoming a better professional educator is to do more research about different ways that students learn. I think that an effective educator is a person that is constantly looking for more opportunities to learn about ones students' learning abilities. As the habit of mind number 12 states, it is important for a good educator to show care for ones students and finds ways of being more receptive and more thoughtful about ways to help ones students to learn. Although, I considered myself to be very open-minded and always willing to listen to constructive feedback and criticism, I still need to improve some of my habits of mind. For example, I need to think more critically and question authority even more. Even though, I do some level of advocacy, I feel that I don't do enough. It is important that I also keep improving my working with peoples' skills. Although, we "help each other and I am very sensitive to my group's need. If I need to go the extra mile to help M or C with their research or anything else, I will" (Learning Objective 3); I feel that my initial approach to working in groups was not appropriate. I realized that contrary to what I thought, "I have a wonderful group. C and M are really trying hard to get the paper done and I cannot be more pleased with their effort. I don't think that I have drawn energy from them and vice versa. We all work in a group and we divide the work accordingly. We respect each other's opinion. We are all very sensitive. For example, this week C was diagnosed with bronchitis, therefore, we decided to postpone our meeting in public and we met online" (Learning Objective 4). It is after this experience that I realized that I also need to continue to learn to keep a critical eye towards ideas and actions. In addition, the best way to keep students interested, especially little ones is to show passion and eagerness (Habit of Mind 9) for learning. As I show passion for what I am teaching, my students will also feel passionate. One of the main characteristics of this course is that I always found "myself always interested in learning new things. Doing research on my argumentative paper is very interesting, especially because all the information available in our topic is relatively current" (Learning Objective 2). Overall, my main goal in order to be a better educator is to continue my growth as an individual through reflection and learning from my own experiences."

"I can apply all of these factors with my students – by facilitating the teaching and allowing time for discovery and exploration in the learning. When selecting group members, I can guide students through the team building process by providing support and receiving feedback from the group members. I can work with my students at being patient and supportive in all aspects of the instruction."

"Week 3 I will apply what I have learned to my high achieving students who tend to get frustrated when they do not immediately understand what were are covering or do not see the big picture.

Week 4 I will apply what I have learned to all of my students to give them the security of knowing that I will follow through with them no matter how long it takes.

Week 5 I think I can apply these habits to everyone I lead. By being a resource for their success I too become successful."

"The first application that comes to mind is being able to make the best out of any situation-such as FCAT lessons. I don't like to teach to the test, the kids don't like it, and their parents don't either. I see thought that I can make the lessons as fun and educational as possible even if we are stuck in a situation where learning is not taking place as it should be."

"I was introduced for the first time to John Dewey. I learned that Dewey is one of the most important education philosophers of all time. His ideas about the individual and ones link to society are essential to ones development as a responsible person. I also learned that his idea about growing through direct experience with materials in the world is the way that I teach my preschoolers. One of the main aspects of my curriculum is to make students participate in their own learning by giving them the opportunity to select and activity and provide them with the materials so they can work on it. I will re-enforce my curriculum and provide my students with more hands on experience. I have realized after my journey in this course, it is essential to provide students with experiences so they could grow. The younger a teacher provides experiences to students the better. Now, I understand how important the grade I teach is. Pre-K is the beginning of the students' learning journey; it is at this stage that they learn what will serve them for the rest of their life."

"I feel like as a teacher I already am a leader for the students. It makes me think I may one day want to be an administrator to lead teachers. My positive group experience can be applied to teaching by allowing more group learning opportunities for my students."

"I have already begun to apply some of these methods to my teaching. In hindsight I think I have always taken a Dewey approach to teaching. I think I have gained the most from this course in my new found ability to argue why I am taking this approach as oppose to another. I think I can better explain why my method is more conducive to teaching my students."

Administrative Transfer

"I believe that when you are an administrator many times you are not open to staff's opinions or suggestions. You are more inclined to make decisions based on your own opinions or ideas (at least that is what I see here at FIU). Which leads me on to say that it is vital that one keeps an open-mind when dealing with large groups. I'm not saying that you have to take into account everything that is being shared with you but it is always good to listen to what it is that your staff is feeling or thinking. Interdependency is also a key factor when being an administrator. I believe that when you are running a department your staff feels more at ease when they know they are contributing something to a whole. It would make the staff work better (in most situations). It makes them feel as part of a mini society."

"I have acquired knowledge on philosophical ideas which I am sure will help me become a good administrator. I am not a teacher, I taught for one year in Georgia. I would like to apply my knowledge I gained in this class to become a better administrator. I am setting my goal to finish my master's degree. I have been lucky, to have Professor Erskine as my professor for this class. I have learned to follow the steps of this educative journey. I have learned to be patient, to listen careful, to read instruction, to be in constant journal writing my experiences of what I learned today. It is a lot of work, but I always find time to do my work for this class. I enjoyed and learned through the five-steps of this journey. Upon completion of my master's degree, I will find another job at as an administrator where I will put to work the knowledge I have gained in this class, for sure."

"All of the learning that took place can be used professionally. The lesson of group work can be applied to me and my colleagues in the very busy registrar office. Learning skills to facilitate an appreciation for every member of the group and to listen and allow others an opportunity is essential. Specifically, I can perhaps persuade the appeals committee to do their best work and to be open to suggestions from their colleagues. Being an administrator, incorporates not only working individually but also in groups. After taking this class I am not hesitant anymore to work with other people. I have learned that to have a cooperative group, the first thing one needs to do is set up rules, which all group members should abide from. After that, a meeting schedule needs be set during which time all group members should present themselves. To always keep in touch with one another, everyone in the group should share their email addresses and phone numbers with the other members."

"My goal is to work as a director of campus life. I love to inspire others to help them reach their highest potential. One way that I can help them do that is by reflection. By understanding the reasons why they do things or the way things happen. I feel that if you can understand you are more likely to make that change you want to. Through reflection you can get a better understanding of yourself and others. You can solve problems which people go through all the time. I want to express to my students the value of reflection and how powerful it can be. I agree with Dewey about the concept of learning through your experiences. I feel experiences are everything, but if you don't reflect upon them then they are worthless. We must always be learning, and I mean in all aspects of life. I feel that every day you can learn something new to different extents. One must just realize that they are learning something. Whether it's from themselves or others actions."

"Since I want to become an administrator I feel that now I will be more comfortable when relying on others. Before this class I knew as an AP or a principal I would drastically have to change from doing most things alone in my classroom to relying on others. I told myself I would get used to this idea but that I would never really enjoy it. Now, I think the process may be enjoyable if I bring the same enthusiasm I did to our group work to future learning community endeavors."

"At my current position at Miami Dade College, I wear two hats that of an Academic Advisor and that of a Student Success Professor, which mounts to my curious title of Intervention Specialist. My undergraduate degree is in Psychology with a plus 60 graduate credits in the area of Clinical Psychology and Rehabilitation Counseling but with no education course until now. After teaching at the college for two years, I really did not feel I was trained well as an educator but pretty much thrown in there to fly by the seat of my pants so to speak. Although, I have been successful I have never been satisfied completely with my skill as an educator. I have learned a great deal about the process of learning and will incorporate many principles set forth by John Dewey in my curriculum. Although, I was already incorporating reflection, and active learning, I will step it up to the next level. Also, I will change the class project to a group project to allow them to develop their interpersonal and interdependence skills in learning communities. As an Academic Advisor, I will suggest more philosophy courses than I previously encouraged."

"As a teacher, and especially as a future administrator, I will have to learn to reflect before acting. I know that I can't let my impulses or feelings guide me when making a decision, especially during delicate or complicated situations. I will have to exercise control and take the time to reflect and connect the dots before taking a stand. I want to project confidence, maturity, and a sense of control. Acting impulsively will only make me look flaky, unorganized, and untrustworthy of my actions to my peers and staff."

Personal Transfer

"All habits of mind presented here, are great strategies to self-grow as a professional educator. In my case as an administrator, listening well to others and caring for others is a habit I should always practice, being that my philosophy is to always help the student in any possible way. I should also work on communicating well, my thoughts and ideas to others."

"Making an agenda to organize better my time and release the pressure not to jeopardize my performance, reading more about the subjects and always reflect about my day to make the next one better."

"Believe it or not I intend to review the 12 habits of mind on this template at least once a month, like they were from Ben Franklin himself. I can truthfully say that they have helped me grow as a person and an individual."

"Knowing not that I do have a difficult time expressing exactly what I am thinking I will be more mindful when I speak to others as an educator and as an administrator. I know I need to develop strategies that will enable me to better communicate. For example, next year as a teacher I wm going to set up a website similar to black board that will allow my students the opportunity to ask me question on topics they was me to clarify. I am going to start there and see where that takes me."

"I believe that I must continue to master the art of being mindful in order to become a professional researcher. I don't see myself as an educator, but more as a voice for children who are underprivileged. I must take the time to understand those who I want to help and why. Most importantly, I need to be able to work more effectively with other people. If I want to reach the masses in the future I need to be able to work more efficiently with other people who might not hold the same views that I do, or in other words I need to be more understanding to others. Only because others do not hold the same views that I do does not mean that I can't learn something from them."

"I have several goals that I which to pursue for professional and personal growth. First, I want to complete my Master's Degree in Higher Education Administration, so that I can obtain a higher administrative position and at the same time this will allow me to teach social science courses in the area of Psychology. College positions that I am interested in would be the Chairperson for the Social Science department or the Dean of Student Services. Personally, I would like to take undergraduate classes in philosophy and Miami Dade College offers: Introduction to Logic, Introduction to Philosophy, Introduction to Eastern Philosophy, Critical Thinking & Ethics and Political Philosophy."

"I will try to listen more to others and be more observant of their behaviors. I will reflect more not only on my own actions but on what my students are telling me through their actions and words."

"One strategy for self-growth would be to learn to be more interdependent in my current position. If I make it a habit in doing so in a way that it is viewed as being constructive then it will lead me to be a better-rounded administrator. I would know how to interact with my employees and making sure that my staff feels as part of a team and not just as robots working in a factory. I will begin to apply many of the learned items in my daily life as well as my professional life."

"To live in society and in order to have a good life we must reflect and think before acting. I can apply on being more disciplined and knowing my limits and necessities in many areas of my life. I am also learning to complete my tasks in advance not to have so much pressure on the activities I have to complete and not to jeopardize my performance."

"I would apply what I learned above to advocating on never giving up when having a hard time and struggling with something. If others can do it so can you too! In addition I believe persistence and patience is essential for all situations in life. I would also advocate good communication in all instances in life."

"Though I am not in school to be a teacher or administrator, I learned that in order to be a good researcher, one must be able to come up with a valid argument. It is important, I learned, that when introducing a research question (or problem) one must be clear and free of bias when conducting a research experiment."

Statistical Evidence of Change in Habits of Mind

So, did the experience in EDF 6608 enhance and nurture reflective intelligence and its related habits of mind? Paired t-test results on the Habits of Mind Self-Rating Scale (pre-/post-) show statistical significant differences on, at least, three of the habits of mind: being thoughtful, persisting, and thinking interdependently.

Habit of Mind: Being Thoughtful-withhold value judgment about an idea until understanding is achieved *(manage impulsivity) versus* blurt out the first answer that comes to mind *(act without forethought)*.

	Group One	Group Two
Mean	3.36	4.14
Standard Deviation	0.85	0.77
N	22	22

t=3.2659 df=21 p=0.0037 (difference is statistically significant)

Habit of Mind: Work to See Things Through-persevere on the task even though the resolution is not immediately apparent *(persisting) versus* write down and/or say things just to be done with the task at hand quickly *(despair easily)*

	Group One	Group Two
Mean	3.86	4.41
Standard Deviation	0.99	0.73
N	22	22

t=2.3238 df=21 p=0.0303 (difference is statistically significant)

Habit of Mind: Being a Cooperative Team Member-contribute to group work by being able to work and learn from others in reciprocal situations *(thinking interdependently) versus* not contribute to group work either by being a "job hog" or by letting others do all the work *(prefer solitude)*

	Group One	Group Two
Mean	3.86	4.64
Standard Deviation	0.89	0.66
N	22	22

t=3.1465 df=21 p=0.0049 (difference is statistically significant)

Candidates showed a statistically significant difference between their pre- and post-journey self-ratings on the above three habits of mind. These data suggest that candidates perceived significant changes in their thinking before acting, in their striving to clarify and understand what they heard, in their, in their sticking to the group paper task until it was completed, and in their drawing energy from others and seeking reciprocity.

The results indicate that class members came to see themselves as being more thoughtful, being persistent in working to see things through, and being more cooperative as a result of their experience in EDF 6608.

Other Evidence of Perceived Change in Habits of Mind

Some positive changes in the mean pre- and post-Self Rating scores while not statistically significant were also indicative of changes in candidates' perceptions with regard to their conduct and the habits of mind.

Habit of Mind: Transfer learning to new situation-begin new task by making connections to prior experience and knowledge (*applying past knowledge to new situations*) *versus* begin new task as if it were being approached for the first time and make no connection to prior experience (*does not transfer knowledge*)

	Group One	Group Two
Mean	4.23	4.50
Standard Deviation	0.97	0.67
N	22	22

Habit of Mind: Care for and listen well to others-devote mental energy to understanding others' thoughts and feelings (*listening with understanding and empathy*) *versus* not paying close attention to what is being said beneath the words (*hears but does not listen*)

	Group One	Group Two
Mean	4.18	4.36
Standard Deviation	0.91	0.79
N	22	22

Habit of Mind: Think and communicate with clarity and precision-use clear language and thinking in both written and oral forms (*thinking and communicating with clarity and precision*) *versus* use fuzzy language and thinking in both written and oral forms (*vague and fuzzy thinking and writing*)

	Group One	Group Two
Mean	3.95	4.09
Standard Deviation	1.21	0.61
N	22	22

Habit of Mind: Act on the basis of own initiative-be more interested in being challenged
by the process of finding the answer than in just knowing the answer is correct (*take responsible risks*) *versus* be more interested in knowing the answer is correct than being
challenged by the process of finding the answer (*fears failure*)

	Group One	Group Two
Mean	4.05	4.18
Standard Deviation	1.17	0.85
N	22	22

Habit of Mind: Show curiosity and passion about learning-have fun figuring things out
(*responding with wonderment and awe*) *versus* perceive thinking as hard work and recoil
from situations that demand too much of it (*no passion about learning, inquiry and mastering* work)

	Group One	Group Two
Mean	4.09	4.14
Standard Deviation	0.97	0.83
N	22	22

On the other hand, there were changes in pre-/post-Self Rating mean scores that suggested a reassessment of perceptions about candidates' conduct.

Habit of Mind: Think about own thinking-reflect on experience (*thinking flexibly*) *versus*
not take time to reflect on experience (*unthoughtful*)

	Group One	Group Two
Mean	4.36	4.18
Standard Deviation	0.95	0.80
N	22	22

Habit of Mind: Being open-minded-be open-minded (*thinking flexibly*) *versus* (resist
changing mind even in light of new data (*close-minded*)

	Group One	Group Two
Mean	4.27	4.18
Standard Deviation	1.03	0.91
N	22	22

Habit of Mind: Take time to check over work-find reworking task acceptable because of
more interest in excellent work than in expediency (*striving for accuracy*) *versus* more
anxious to complete task than to take time to check accuracy and precision (*no pride in
work*)

	Group One	Group Two
Mean	4.05	4.00
Standard Deviation	1.09	0.93
N	22	22

There was no change in mean scores on the following habit of mind.

Habit of Mind: Adopt a critical eye toward ideas and actions-adopt a questioning attitude (*questioning and posing problems*) *versus* avoid asking questions to fill in unknown gaps (*unquestioning*)

	Group One	Group Two
Mean	4.09	4.09
Standard Deviation	1.02	0.87
N	22	22

LESSONS LEARNED FROM THE EXPERIENCE

"You cannot measure process-oriented outcomes using product-oriented assessment techniques"

So, what may have contributed to the enhanced awareness of and growth in habits of mind of candidates in EDF 6608? Evidence in the previous chapter indicates that candidates did learn from the experience. They did grow, and they did modify their actions based on prior experience. They even extended and deepened their interest in learning by being more thoughtful, more persistent in working to see things through, and more cooperative in thinking interdependently. They enhanced life for themselves individually and for the collective class EDF 6608. More so, they began to show a desire, inclination and/or sensitivity to demonstrate habits of mind. The lessons learned from this experience reinforce the words of Costa and Kallick (2008):

> We need to find ways of assessing and reporting growth in the Habits of Mind....Gathering evidence of performance and growth in the Habits of Mind requires 'kid watching.' As students interact with real-life, day-to-day problems in school, at home, on the playground, alone, and with friends, teaching teams and other adults can collect anecdotes and examples of written and visual expressions that reveal students' increasingly skillful, voluntary, and spontaneous use of these Habits of Mind in diverse situations and circumstances (p. xxii).

Lesson One

Candidates bring habits that predispose them to act in this way or that way, that is, motivate them to act, so it is critical to start the learning experience by getting candidates to think about their own thinking, in other words, to focus on self-regulated learning, and their being mindful. According to Ritchhart (2002) self-regulated learning can be described as "the learner's effectiveness in motivating, directing, and monitoring his or her own learning. This construct is dispositional because it requires not only the cultivation of specific abilities but also the effective use of those abilities in the learning situation" (p. 40). In fact, "To avoid mindlessness and achieve mindfulness, one must be aware of and move beyond one's preexisting categories, automatic responses to situations, and the personal perspective one brings to new encounters" (Ritchhart, 2002, p. 40).

One can get a sense of the struggle with mindfulness for some candidates in the course:

"This journey has not been an easy one. I have found myself plenty of times being uninterested in writing my reflections. At times it felt as if they were a waste of time and that
more focus should have been put on composing the argumentative paper."

"I want to be challenged but I am finding it difficult to find a starting point. I feel like we
are being thrown to so many different directions that I am missing the concept. Erskine
wants us to start off with a "what ought to be question". Okay, so we are doing this to
help us come up with a moral/philosophical problem. I get that. It just seems like this
process is not necessary. I guess maybe that's because I have not totally understood the
concept. I'm hoping that if I continue to push forward and be open minded to a new
learning process, that all of a sudden my light bulb will go off. I am defiantly challenged.
I'm not going to lie, I also feel a little frustrated because it's not coming all together like I
would like."

"As an important part of my graduate course, EDF 6608 my professor (Dr. Dottin) has
asked me to reflect on the "journey" of my learning as I go along the process. I have
learned that this is an integral part of this very different type of learning experience,
where there this no midterm and final; it is almost like landing on a different type of
learning planet, I am definitely no longer in Kansas. However, this was justified by the
professor in a way that pierced my psyche like a knife, midterm and final exams are
merely regurgitation of information, which has little value if one wants to learn in an im-
pactful, higher order thinking manner. The idea of no final/midterm definitely took some
getting use to but was justified in the name of thinking, reflecting, changing behavior, in
short a process that is outside of the norm. I have often found myself thinking outside of
the norms and getting punished in some way in the end, which I guess makes me cau-
tious. However, it comforts me that it seems the professor is paralleling the learning journey to what the final process will be; action is imitating thought/ideas and vice versa."

The experience in EDF 6608 reaffirmed that habits operate subconsciously and
cannot be changed by will power. Take for example, the candidate who indicated the
following at the start of the educational journey:

"My first day of class (I could not attend the first day) was very confusing. I had read the
professor's emails and it contained terms foreign to me. The syllabus was called a "map".
I've used maps before. I have a GPS now, so a map seems archaic in these times, but
maps have been useful to me in the past. I used on my way from Gainesville to Jacksonville in college. There was a clear distinction between that map and our "map". The map I
used to get to Jacksonville had a clear beginning and end for me. I started in one place
and ended in another. But, where is our "map" taking us? What kind of "journey" is the
professor talking about? I was lost before I even looked closely at the map."

The candidate brought to the learning experience the idea that learning was simply a
matter of being directed from one point to another (the GPS model). However, in undergoing the self-regulated learning experience in EDF 6608 that called forth independent
thought and deliberative inquiry (into seeing where one has been and anticipate where

one is going on the journey-the map), the candidate exhibited an epiphany that suggested developmental growth and an awareness of the habit of mind of being thoughtful.

> "I prejudged this journey before I got a full understanding of it. Allowing the professor to explain his reasoning and withhold judgment was/is a key indicator that I am starting to the thoughtful in actions."

Indirect means to change habits did work in the above example, and the candidate's mindfulness and thoughtfulness was enhanced.

Lesson Two

Candidates' focus on the Habits of Mind will be enhanced if the cognitive task on which they are working is designed to so that they deepen their thinking about the subject at each level of the task as they process material to meet the expectations of the cognitive task (Costa & Kallick, 2008, p. 51). The "backward course design" (Wiggins & McTighe, 2005) used in EDF 6608 enabled candidates to be challenged by the authentic problem posing argumentative paper task and to give meaning to that work by drawing upon the Habits of Mind. Candidates not only had to use the Habits of Mind to succeed in the performance task that was assigned (See Rubric in Chapter 4, and Final Course Evaluation for the Argumentative Paper in Chapter 5), but they also learned that success was ensured by applying those habits mindfully (Costa & Kallick, 2008, p. 51). The problem posing environment of the course facilitated intelligent conduct in that candidates were attending to and drawing on, in particular, meta-cognitive strategies of being thoughtful, experiencing the effect of persisting on the argumentative paper, and to thinking interdependently. Candidates' application of thinking to things already known (the course content and related process skills) for the purpose of improving social conditions (to act on the outcomes of inquiry into the following: Should the arts be a stable aspect of an education for a democratic society? Should teachers' salaries be based on their students' performance on standardized tests? Should the children of undocumented immigrants who entered the U.S. illegally, and have attended and finished High School, be afforded the same in-state tuition and financial aid benefits at our state universities, as students who are citizens and or legal residents? Should an educator change a student's grade in order to accommodate the student's wants and interests? Should schools attend to the individual needs of the learner or only to state policy? Should the carrying of handguns on K-12 school facilities by teachers and administrators be considered compatible with the goals of education in a democratic society? Should students be groups homogenously in classrooms based on sex or should students be grouped heterogeneously based on the principles of democracy?) nurtured both intellectual and social habits that would render candidates' conduct more intelligent.

The cognitive task, the argumentative paper, pursued through different stages of inquiry helped candidates to move toward a process of internalization of the habits of mind
as they reflected on the use of the Habits of Mind. This reflective process, in the Habits
of Mind Inventory, enabled candidates to think about the transfer of the Habits of Mind in
other situations beyond the course.

The development of the Habits of Mind occurred through inquiry situated and per-
formance-based activities, and the class tasks were consistent with calling forth the requisite habits of mind. Candidates got to experience the conditions by and through which the
Habits of Mind were needed. In other words, the course environment did not reinforce
just getting right answers. Instead, the environment drew candidates into acting in pursuing their own interests while interacting with others in ways that deepened and widened
their social sympathies, and invited candidates to see the interrelatedness of knowledge,
skills and dispositions (habits of mind).

Conclusion

If teacher education programs are going to focus on nurturing and assessing dispositions (The Habits of Mind) then candidates must be provided opportunities to see the
habits of mind, practice them, and receive feedback about their performance vis-à-vis the
Habits of Mind. Some scholars have pointed out that the rush by many teacher education
programs to meet accreditation mandates with regard to "dispositions" has generated a
host of measures for assessing dispositions and very little focus on programs first estab-
lishing some conceptual understanding of the construct, and then teaching candidates
about dispositions (Diez, 2006; Diez, 2007; Sockett, 2009). Generating measures of "dispositions" without first teaching "dispositions" assumes that candidates' internal motivator to guide intelligent conduct will work automatically. In other words, the assumption is
that all candidates will be self-initiated in their awareness, inclination and desire to demonstrate the Habits of Mind. Consequently, one finds many programs using candidates
self-reports about dispositions without teaching the candidates about dispositions.

If the Habits of Mind are the internal compass to making professional conduct more
intelligent, that is, professionals "not only having information but also knowing how to
act on it" (Costa & Kallick, 2008, p. xxii) then the lesson here is that teacher education
programs should facilitate candidates growth in the Habits of Mind by utilizing Ritchhart's suggestion to use external prompts or "triggers" as means to help candidates link
ability and action:

> In our day-to-day work, we often encounter times when we lack inclination, awareness,
> or motivation. When an internal mechanism fails, an external force may step in to assist
> in bridging the gap between ability and action, For example, I have a tendency to leave
> the stove on when I am cooking. I'm quite motivated to turn it off, because I am not eager
> to burn the house down! However, I tend not to be very aware of the burners when I am

not using them. I'm often distracted by the other demands of preparing a meal. Knowing this, my partner regularly prompts me to check the burners before I sit down to dinner. Thus my lack of awareness is compensated for by an external force, a prompt by someone else to check the burners (Ritchhart, 2002, pp. 42, 44).

There are, however, critical elements necessary to enhance external triggers being internalized by candidates. Ritchhart (2002) suggests that the contributing factors include candidates seeing the dispositions [the Habits of Mind], their receiving explicit instruction about [the Habits of Mind], their having opportunities to practice [the Habits of Mind], and their receiving consistent rather than contradictory messages with regard to the Habits of Mind.

The triggers in EDF 6608 were (1) the structure of the learning sessions by objectives which required candidates to acquire content and process skills to use in an inquiry process that evoked the Habits of Mind, and (2) candidates having to reflect on their actions with regard to the Habits of Mind and to write their reflections in the Habits of Mind Inventory. These reflections suggest that the learning environment was engendering instruction about the Habits of Mind.

So, did the candidates' experience in EDF 6608 increase their capacity to solve pedagogical problems, to make informed decisions, and to generate new knowledge in the world of practice? Did the experience generate in them a desire for continued growth? Has their professional conduct been made more intelligent? Have they grown professionally by approaching situations in a certain way that displays a general set of actions associated with the Habits of Mind? While initial observations and candidates' reflections from the course would suggest an affirmative response, a follow-up of candidates in the work place would offer a more detailed empirical answer about whether they are showing the internal motivation (habit) to conduct themselves intelligently, that is, to exercise professional judgment in action.

APPENDIX A SELF-RATING SCALE

SELF RATING SCALE
Developed by Erskine S. Dottin, May 2, 2005 Revised December 19, 2007 These twelve items were adapted from David Hansen (2001) *Exploring the moral heart of teaching* and Arthur Costa & Bena Kallick (2000) *Activating & engaging: Habits of mind.*

Please rate yourself on each of the following habits of mind/dispositions at one of the levels indicated (place an X in the box to represent your disposition level along the continuum: **5 = consistently to 1 = very little**

NAME:		
adopt a questioning attitude *(questioning and posing problems)*		avoid asking questions to fill in unknown gaps *(unquestioning)*
be open-minded *(thinking flexibly)*		resist changing mind even in light of new data *(closed minded)*
withhold value judgment about an idea until understanding is achieved *(manage impulsivity)*		blurt out the first answer that comes to mind *(acts without forethought)*
persevere on the task even though the resolution is not immediately apparent *(persisting)*		write down and/or say things just to be done with the task at hand quickly *(despairs easily)*
reflect on my experience(s) *(thinking about own thinking)*		not take time to reflect on my experience(s) *(unthoughtful)*
… find reworking task acceptable because more of interest in excellent work than in expediency *(striving for accuracy)*		more anxious to complete task than to take time to check for accuracy and precision *(no pride in work)*
use clear language and thinking in both written and oral forms *(thinking and communicating with clarity and precision)*		use fuzzy language and thinking in both written and oral forms *(vague and fuzzy thinking and writing)*
begin new task by making connections to prior experience and knowledge *(applying past knowledge to new situations)*		begin new task as if it were being approached for the first time and make no connection to prior experience *(does not transfer knowledge)*

have fun figuring things out *(responding with wonderment and awe)*		perceive thinking as hard work and recoil from situations that demand too much of it *(no passion about learning, inquiry and mastering work)*
be more interested in being challenged by the process of finding the answer than in just knowing the answer is correct *(take responsible risks)*		be more interested in knowing the answer is correct than being challenged by the process of finding the answer *(fears failure)*
contribute to group work by being able to work and learn from others in reciprocal situations *(thinking interdependently)*		not contribute to group work either by being a "job hog" or by letting others do all the work *(prefers solitude)*
devote mental energy to understanding others' thoughts and feelings *(listening with understanding and empathy)*		not pay close attention to what is being said beneath the words *(hears but does not listen)*

APPENDIX B HABITS OF MIND INVENTORY

Running Head: PERSONAL REFLECTIONS

Habits of Mind Inventory

Name: INSERT WHEN COMPLETED

Florida International University

Submitted to: Dr. Erskine Dottin

Date: INSERT WHEN COMPLETED

This Inventory was developed by Erskine S. Dottin 14810 SW 149th Avenue, Miami, Florida 33196 (Summer 2007) as a tool to facilitate the assessment of habits of mind (dispositions) of professional educators.

Table of Contents

11. Be a cooperative team member ....

12. Care for others and listen well to others ....

1. **Habit of Mind**
    Adopt a critical eye toward ideas and actions
adopt a questioning attitude (questioning and posing problems) VERSUS avoid asking questions to fill in unknown gaps (unquestioning)

REFLECT ON YOUR CONDUCT AFTER EACH OF THE FOLLOWING LEARNING OBJECTIVES IN THE COURSE, AND PROVIDE WRITTEN RESPONSES TO THE QUESTIONS BELOW: State the situation during the respective Learning Objective that caused you to be aware of your demonstrating or not demonstrating the habit of mind. Describe the activity, its circumstances, for example, who was involved? What were the circumstances? When and where did the event occur? State whether your analysis of the activity provides any reflective insights about why you did what you did or did not do with respect to learning in the course? Can you use any educational theory to interpret the experience? Have you gained insights from the experience that have or will improve your thoughtfulness?

LEARNING OBJECTIVE #1
Did you find yourself asking questions to enable you to fill in the gap between what you knew and did not know? Did you find yourself posing questions about alternative positions or points of view? Did you find yourself probing into the causes of things or did you just accept things as they were? Did you find yourself just posing questions that required a yes or no answer or did you pose more complex questions?

LEARNING OBJECTIVE #4
Did you find yourself asking questions to enable you to fill in the gap between what you knew and did not know? Did you find yourself posing questions about alternative positions or points of view? Did you find yourself probing into the causes of things or did you just accept things as they were? Did you find yourself just posing questions that required a yes or no answer or did you pose more complex questions?

2. **Habit of Mind**
    Being open-minded
Be open-minded *(thinking flexibly) VERSUS* resist changing mind even in light of new data *(closed minded)*

REFLECT ON YOUR CONDUCT AFTER EACH OF THE FOLLOWING LEARNING OBJECTIVES IN THE COURSE, AND PROVIDE WRITTEN RESPONSES TO THE QUESTIONS BELOW: State the situation during the respective Learning Objective that caused you to be aware of your demonstrating or not demonstrating the habit of mind. Describe the activity, its circumstances, for example, who was involved? What were the circumstances? When and where did the event occur? State whether your

analysis of the activity provides any reflective insights about why you did what you did or did not do with respect to learning in the course? Can you use any educational theory to interpret the experience? Have you gained insights from the experience that have or will improve your thoughtfulness?

LEARNING OBJECTIVE #4
Did you find yourself changing your mind based on new credible data? Did you find yourself always wanting to approach things in the same way (the way to which you have become most accustomed)? Did you find yourself being able to perceive things from perspectives other than your own? Did you find yourself being able to tolerate ambiguity up to a point?

3. **Habit of Mind**
   Being thoughtful in actions
Withhold value judgment about an idea until understanding is achieved *(manage impulsivity)* *VERSUS* blurt out the first answer that comes to mind *(acts without forethought)*

REFLECT ON YOUR CONDUCT AFTER EACH OF THE FOLLOWING LEARNING OBJECTIVES IN THE COURSE, AND PROVIDE WRITTEN RESPONSES TO THE QUESTIONS BELOW: State the situation during the respective Learning Objective that caused you to be aware of your demonstrating or not demonstrating the habit of mind. Describe the activity, its circumstances, for example, who was involved? What were the circumstances? When and where did the event occur? State whether your analysis of the activity provides any reflective insights about why you did what you did or did not do with respect to learning in the course? Can you use any educational theory to interpret the experience? Have you gained insights from the experience that have or will improve your thoughtfulness?

LEARNING OBJECTIVE #1
Did you find yourself acting and then thinking or thinking before acting? Did you find yourself striving to clarify and understand what you hear, read, etc.? Did you find yourself jumping to offer an opinion about something that you did not understand fully? Did you consider different possibilities before taking action? Did you find yourself always accepting the first idea that came to mind?

LEARNING OBJECTIVE #3
Did you find yourself acting and then thinking or thinking before acting? Did you find yourself striving to clarify and understand what you hear, read, etc.? Did you find yourself jumping to offer an opinion about something that you did not understand fully? Did you consider different possibilities before taking action? Did you find yourself always accepting the first idea that came to mind?

LEARNING OBJECTIVE #4
Did you find yourself acting and then thinking or thinking before acting? Did you find yourself striving to clarify and understand what you hear, read, etc.? Did you find your

*self jumping to offer an opinion about something that you did not understand fully? Did
you consider different possibilities before taking action? Did you find yourself always accepting the first idea that came to mind?*

4. <u>Habit of Mind</u>
   <u>Work to see things through</u>

persevere on the task even though the resolution is not immediately apparent *(persisting)*
VERSUS write down and/or say things just to be done with the task at hand quickly *(despairs
easily)*

**REFLECT ON YOUR CONDUCT AFTER EACH OF THE FOLLOWING LEARN-
ING OBJECTIVES IN THE COURSE, AND PROVIDE WRITTEN RESPONSES TO
THE QUESTIONS BELOW:** State the situation during the respective Learning Objective that caused you to be aware of your demonstrating or not demonstrating the habit of
mind. Describe the activity, its circumstances, for example, who was involved? What
were the circumstances? When and where did the event occur? State whether your
analysis of the activity provides any reflective insights about why you did what you did
or did not do with respect to learning in the course? Can you use any educational theory
to interpret the experience? Have you gained insights from the experience that have or
will improve your thoughtfulness?

LEARNING OBJECTIVE #2
*Did you find yourself wanting to stick to the group paper or other class tasks until it is
(they are) completed or wanting to give up? Did you find yourself setting up a systematic
system to guide you in completing the paper or other class tasks? Did you find yourself
giving up easily when the answer to something was not immediately known? Did you find
yourself staying on focus throughout the learning experience or being easily distracted?*

5. <u>Habit of Mind</u>
   <u>Think about own thinking</u>

Reflect on my experience(s) (thinking about own thinking) VERSUS not take time to reflect
on my experience(s) (unthoughtful)

**PROVIDE WRITTEN RESPONSES TO THE QUESTIONS BELOW [EACH WEEK]
AS YOU MOVE THROUGH THE EDUCATIONAL JOURNEY IN THE COURSE.**
State the situation in the course that caused you to be aware of your demonstrating or
not demonstrating the habit of mind. Describe the activity, its circumstances, for example, who was involved? What were the circumstances? When and where did the event
occur? State whether your analysis of the activity provides any reflective insights about
why you did what you did or did not do with respect to learning in the course? Can you
use any educational theory to interpret the experience? Have you gained insights from
the experience that have or will improve your thoughtfulness?

LEARNING OBJECTIVE #3

Did you find yourself planning for, reflecting on, and evaluating the quality of your own thinking? Did you find yourself being increasingly aware of your actions on others? Did you find yourself developing and using mental maps or rehearsing before you performed an action? Did you find yourself reflecting on your actions (what you did)? Did you find yourself usually wondering about why you were doing what you were doing? Did you find yourself being able to explain your decision-making process on matters?

LEARNING OBJECTIVE #4

Did you find yourself planning for, reflecting on, and evaluating the quality of your own thinking? Did you find yourself being increasingly aware of your actions on others? Did you find yourself developing and using mental maps or rehearsing before you performed an action? Did you find yourself reflecting on your actions (what you did)? Did you find yourself usually wondering about why you were doing what you were doing? Did you find yourself being able to explain your decision-making process on matters?

LEARNING OBJECTIVE #5

Did you find yourself planning for, reflecting on, and evaluating the quality of your own thinking? Did you find yourself being increasingly aware of your actions on others? Did you find yourself developing and using mental maps or rehearsing before you performed an action? Did you find yourself reflecting on your actions (what you did)? Did you find yourself usually wondering about why you were doing what you were doing? Did you find yourself being able to explain your decision-making process on matters?

6. **Habit of Mind**
   Take time to check over work

Find reworking task acceptable because more of interest in excellent work than in expediency (striving for accuracy) VERSUS more anxious to complete task than to take time to check for accuracy and precision (no pride in work)

REFLECT ON YOUR CONDUCT AFTER EACH OF THE FOLLOWING LEARNING OBJECTIVES IN THE COURSE, AND PROVIDE WRITTEN RESPONSES TO THE QUESTIONS BELOW: State the situation during the respective Learning Objective that caused you to be aware of your demonstrating or not demonstrating the habit of mind. Describe the activity, its circumstances, for example, who was involved? What were the circumstances? When and where did the event occur? State whether your analysis of the activity provides any reflective insights about why you did what you did or did not do with respect to learning in the course? Can you use any educational theory to interpret the experience? Have you gained insights from the experience that have or will improve your thoughtfulness?

LEARNING OBJECTIVE #2

Did you find yourself wanting to produce excellent work? Did you find yourself checking over what you produced? Did you find yourself wanting to perfect your work? Did you find yourself holding to high standards in any work you produced?

7. **Habit of Mind**
    Think and communicate with clarity and precision

Use clear language and thinking in both written and oral forms *(thinking and communicating with clarity and precision) VERSUS* use fuzzy language and thinking in both written and oral forms *(vague and fuzzy thinking and writing)*

REFLECT ON YOUR CONDUCT AFTER EACH OF THE FOLLOWING LEARN-ING OBJECTIVES IN THE COURSE, AND PROVIDE WRITTEN RESPONSES TO THE QUESTIONS BELOW: State the situation during the respective Learning Objec-tive that caused you to be aware of your demonstrating or not demonstrating the habit of mind. Describe the activity, its circumstances, for example, who was involved? What were the circumstances? When and where did the event occur? State whether your analysis of the activity provides any reflective insights about why you did what you did or did not do with respect to learning in the course? Can you use any educational theory to interpret the experience? Have you gained insights from the experience that have or will improve your thoughtfulness?

LEARNING OBJECTIVE #2
Did you find yourself trying to be clear in your writing and speaking? Did you find your-self using fuzzy language and thinking? Did you find yourself using precise language and defining terms and ideas clearly? Did you find yourself using good thinking skills and logic?

8. **Habit of Mind**
    Transfer learning to new situation

begin new task by making connections to prior experience and knowledge (applying past knowledge to new situations) VERSUS begin new task as if it were being approached for the first time and make no connection to prior experience (does not transfer knowledge)

REFLECT ON YOUR CONDUCT AFTER EACH OF THE FOLLOWING LEARN-ING OBJECTIVES IN THE COURSE, AND PROVIDE WRITTEN RESPONSES TO THE QUESTIONS BELOW: State the situation during the respective Learning Objec-tive that caused you to be aware of your demonstrating or not demonstrating the habit of mind. Describe the activity, its circumstances, for example, who was involved? What were the circumstances? When and where did the event occur? State whether your analysis of the activity provides any reflective insights about why you did what you did or did not do with respect to learning in the course? Can you use any educational theory to interpret the experience? Have you gained insights from the experience that have or will improve your thoughtfulness?

LEARNING OBJECTIVE #4
Did you find yourself learning from your experiences? Did you find yourself drawing on past experience to solve present problems (situations)? Did you find yourself approach-ing each new task as though it were the first time? Did you find yourself recalling how you may have solved something in the past that is similar to something on which you

were working? Did you find yourself applying something you learned previously in a new situation?

LEARNING OBJECTIVE #5
Did you find yourself learning from your experiences? Did you find yourself drawing on past experience to solve present problems (situations)? Did you find yourself approaching each new task as though it were the first time? Did you find yourself recalling how you may have solved something in the past that is similar to something on which you were working? Did you find yourself applying something you learned previously in a new situation?

9. **Habit of Mind**
   Show curiosity and passion about learning
Have fun figuring things out *(responding with wonderment and awe) VERSUS* perceive thinking as hard work and recoil from situations that demand too much of it *(no passion about learning, inquiry and mastering work)*

REFLECT ON YOUR CONDUCT AFTER EACH OF THE FOLLOWING LEARNING OBJECTIVES IN THE COURSE, AND PROVIDE WRITTEN RESPONSES TO THE QUESTIONS BELOW: State the situation during the respective Learning Objective that caused you to be aware of your demonstrating or not demonstrating the habit of mind. Describe the activity, its circumstances, for example, who was involved? What were the circumstances? When and where did the event occur? State whether your analysis of the activity provides any reflective insights about why you did what you did or did not do with respect to learning in the course? Can you use any educational theory to interpret the experience? Have you gained insights from the experience that have or will improve your thoughtfulness?

LEARNING OBJECTIVE #1
Did you find yourself being turned on about learning new things? Did you find yourself liking things that required hard thinking? Did you find yourself being curious about ordinary things? Did you find yourself interested in inquiring into how and why things were? Did you find yourself wanting to master what you had to do?

LEARNING OBJECTIVE #2
Did you find yourself being turned on about learning new things? Did you find yourself liking things that required hard thinking? Did you find yourself being curious about ordinary things? Did you find yourself interested in inquiring into how and why things were? Did you find yourself wanting to master what you had to do?

10. **Habit of Mind**
    Act on the basis of own initiative
be more interested in being challenged by the process of finding the answer than in just knowing the answer is correct *(take responsible risks)VERSUS* be more interested in knowing the answer is correct than being challenged by the process of finding the answer *(fears failure)*

**REFLECT ON YOUR CONDUCT AFTER EACH OF THE FOLLOWING LEARN-
ING OBJECTIVES IN THE COURSE, AND PROVIDE WRITTEN RESPONSES TO
THE QUESTIONS BELOW: State the situation during the respective Learning Objective that caused you to be aware of your demonstrating or not demonstrating the habit of
mind. Describe the activity, its circumstances, for example, who was involved? What
were the circumstances? When and where did the event occur? State whether your
analysis of the activity provides any reflective insights about why you did what you did
or did not do with respect to learning in the course? Can you use any educational theory
to interpret the experience? Have you gained insights from the experience that have or
will improve your thoughtfulness?**

LEARNING OBJECTIVE #1
*Did you find yourself wanting to go beyond established limits? Did you find yourself be-
ing comfortable in situations whose outcome were not immediately clear? Did you find
yourself accepting failure as part of your own growth? Did you find yourself accepting
setbacks as challenging and growth producing? Did you find yourself knowing when to
take educated risks and when not to take impulsive risks? Did you find yourself willing to
take a chance in the moment or only after you had calculated all costs? Did you find
yourself only knowing the correct answer or were you challenged by the process of finding the answer?*

11. **Habit of Mind**
    Be a cooperative team member
Contribute to group work by being able to work and learn from others in reciprocal situations
(thinking interdependently) VERSUS not contribute to group work either by being a "job hog"
or by letting others do all the work *(prefers solitude)*

**REFLECT ON YOUR CONDUCT AFTER EACH OF THE FOLLOWING LEARN-
ING OBJECTIVES IN THE COURSE, AND PROVIDE WRITTEN RESPONSES TO
THE QUESTIONS BELOW: State the situation during the respective Learning Objective that caused you to be aware of your demonstrating or not demonstrating the habit of
mind. Describe the activity, its circumstances, for example, who was involved? What
were the circumstances? When and where did the event occur? State whether your
analysis of the activity provides any reflective insights about why you did what you did
or did not do with respect to learning in the course? Can you use any educational theory
to interpret the experience? Have you gained insights from the experience that have or
will improve your thoughtfulness?**

LEARNING OBJECTIVE #1
*Did you find yourself drawing energy from others and seeking reciprocity? Did you find
yourself always preferring solitary work? Did you find yourself being sensitive to the
needs of others? Did you find yourself always wanting to be a job hog; just wanting to do
things only with yourself? Did you find yourself just letting others do all the work for
you? Did you find yourself excited about having to justify and test your ideas on others?
Did you find yourself willing to accept feedback from a critical friend?*

LEARNING OBJECTIVE #2

Did you find yourself drawing energy from others and seeking reciprocity? Did you find yourself always preferring solitary work? Did you find yourself being sensitive to the needs of others? Did you find yourself always wanting to be a job hog; just wanting to do things only with yourself? Did you find yourself just letting others do all the work for you? Did you find yourself excited about having to justify and test your ideas on others? Did you find yourself willing to accept feedback from a critical friend?

LEARNING OBJECTIVE #3

Did you find yourself drawing energy from others and seeking reciprocity? Did you find yourself always preferring solitary work? Did you find yourself being sensitive to the needs of others? Did you find yourself always wanting to be a job hog; just wanting to do things only with yourself? Did you find yourself just letting others do all the work for you? Did you find yourself excited about having to justify and test your ideas on others? Did you find yourself willing to accept feedback from a critical friend?

LEARNING OBJECTIVE #4

Did you find yourself drawing energy from others and seeking reciprocity? Did you find yourself always preferring solitary work? Did you find yourself being sensitive to the needs of others? Did you find yourself always wanting to be a job hog; just wanting to do things only with yourself? Did you find yourself just letting others do all the work for you? Did you find yourself excited about having to justify and test your ideas on others? Did you find yourself willing to accept feedback from a critical friend?

12. **Habit of Mind**
   Care for others and listen well to others
Devote mental energy to understanding others' thoughts and feelings *(listening with understanding and empathy) VERSUS not* paying close attention to what is being said beneath the words *(hears but does not listen)*

PROVIDE WRITTEN RESPONSES TO THE QUESTIONS BELOW [EACH WEEK] AS YOU MOVE THROUGH THE EDUCATIONAL JOURNEY IN THE COURSE. State the situation in the course that caused you to be aware of your demonstrating or not demonstrating the habit of mind. Describe the activity, its circumstances, for example, who was involved? What were the circumstances? When and where did the event occur? State whether your analysis of the activity provides any reflective insights about why you did what you did or did not do with respect to learning in the course? Can you use any educational theory to interpret the experience? Have you gained insights from the experience that have or will improve your thoughtfulness?

LEARNING OBJECTIVE #4

Did you find yourself speaking when others were speaking or did you always listen carefully when others were speaking? Did you paraphrase what you heard others say and accurately expressed what was said? Did you find yourself attending carefully to what oth-

ers said beneath their words? Did you hold in abeyance your judgments and opinions so you could listen to another person's thoughts and ideas?

REFLECTIONS [Thinking about your own thinking and behavior and reinforcing self-regulation skills]

Describe what you learned about yourself:

How might you apply what you learned above to your becoming/being a teacher, administrator, or other school professional?.:

REFLECTING ON YOUR GROWTH
Did you grow in any of the habits of mind (please be specific)? Please provide evidence from your inventory to support your assertion(s):

GOALS FOR CONTINUED GROWTH

Were there habits of mind in which you did not grow (please be specific)? Please provide evidence to support your assertion(s):

What goals/strategies will you set for your self-growth (in becoming/being a professional educator) vis-à-vis the habits of mind?

This Inventory was developed by Erskine S. Dottin 14810 SW 149ᵗʰ Avenue, Miami, Florida 33196 (Summer 2007) as a tool to facilitate the assessment of habits of mind (dispositions) of professional educators.

APPENDIX C MEETING STANDARDS TEMPLATE

EDF 6608 SOCIAL, HISTORICAL, AND PHILOSOPHICAL FOUNDATIONS OF EDUCATION
Names of Candidates in Learning Community:

The following is our attempt to show how the artifact we produced in EDF 6608 Social, Historical and Philosophical Foundations of Education (an analytical/argumentative paper) and the knowledge, skills and dispositions we acquired in learning to produce the foregoing artifact are consistent with the knowledge, skills and dispositions required in Institutional, State, and Professional Standards below. The Standards are outlined on the right and we state whether we think we have met the standards or not and provide support for our conclusion through explanations of and reflections on our learning. Our explanations and reflections will relate our acquired knowledge, skills and dispositions to the knowledge, skills, etc. in each standard. We will reflect on how we acquired the necessary competencies (especially the FEAP's – State of Florida Standards) by describing circumstances and situations in which we experienced the competency; by explaining what we did in the learning context; the results of our learning; and how in going through the foregoing we have demonstrated the required competencies in the standards.

STANDARDS	Institutional Standards (College Outcome(s)) –
	What do the College of Education standards require?
	The standards require that you be a:
	Steward of the Discipline
	Know the content and engage in cross-disciplinary activities to ensure breadth and depth of knowledge.
	Reflective Inquirer
	Reflect on practice and change approaches based on own insights.
	Reflect on practice with the goal of continuous improvement.
	Think critically about issues through a form of inquiry that investigates dilemmas and problems and seek resolutions that benefit all involved.
	Mindful Educator
	Being analytical; managing impulsivity; persisting; thinking about own thinking; communicating accurately; being inquisitive; taking responsible risks; being open-minded; striving for accuracy; applying past knowledge to new situations; thinking interdependently; showing a sense of care for others.

| REFLECTIONS ON LEARNING | **INSERT (describe) THE GROUP'S COLLECTIVE REFLECTION ON WHAT GROUP MEMBERS LEARNED FROM THE EXPERIENCE IN EACH RESPECTIVE LEARNING OBJECTIVE AND THE INSIGHTS GAINED** [Describe what you actually learned FROM the ACTIVITIES IN WHICH YOU PARTICIPATED, and Describe how what you learned is linked to [indicative of] ANY THING called for in the above Institutional Standards

Learning Objective #1
To formulate a moral, philosophical problem question, and prepare a brief written introduction to the problem question by contrasting the pros and cons in the problem and by laying out the paper's components.

Insert reflection here:

Learning Objective #2
To use research information effectively to write a literature review

Insert reflection here:

Learning Objective #3
To lay out the structure(s) of arguments

Insert reflection here:

Learning Objective #4
To use ideas from readings as support to justify an ideological and philosophical argument.

Insert reflection here:

Learning Objective #5
To judge how the value judgments in the arguments will help to solve the problem in schools today.

Insert reflection here: |

STANDARDS	**State Standards (Florida Educator Accomplished Practice(s)**
	What do the State (FEAP's) standard require?
	The standards require the following:
	Accomplished Practice #2: Communication – uses effective communication: active listening; constructive feedback; individual and group inquiry strategies.
	Accomplished Practice #3: Continuous Improvement – engages in life-long learning and self-reflection: demonstrates respect for diverse perspectives, ideas, and options; works as a member of a learning community; learns from peers; shows evidence of self-reflection.
	Accomplished Practice # 4 Critical Thinking – utilizes critical understanding of educational thought and practice: shows ability to think critically and creatively; uses higher-order thinking skills.
	Accomplished Practice #6 Ethics – habits that render intelligent professional conduct: demonstrates moral sensibilities: exhibits moral attributes essential for effective professional practice.
	(locate the State Standards at http://www.firn.edu/doe/dpe/publications.htm)
REFLECTIONS ON LEARNING	**INSERT (describe) THE GROUP'S COLLECTIVE REFLECTION ON WHAT GROUP MEMBERS LEARNED FROM THE EXPERIENCE IN EACH RESPECTIVE LEARNING OBJECTIVE AND THE INSIGHTS GAINED** [Describe what you actually learned FROM the ACTIVITIES IN WHICH YOU PARTICIPATED, and Describe how what you learned is linked to [indicative of] ANY THING called for in the above Institutional Standards
	Learning Objective #1
	To formulate a moral, philosophical problem question, and prepare a brief written introduction to the problem question by contrasting the pros and cons in the problem and by laying out the paper's components.
	Insert reflection here:
	Learning Objective #2
	To use research information effectively to write a literature review
	Insert reflection here:
	Learning Objective #3
	To lay out the structure(s) of arguments
	Insert reflection here:
	Learning Objective #4
	To use ideas from readings as support to justify an ideological and philosophical argument.
	Insert reflection here:
	Learning Objective #5
	To judge how the value judgments in the arguments will help to solve the problem in schools today.
	Insert reflection here:

STANDARDS	**National Standards (National Board for Professional Teaching Standards – Accomplished Educator)**
	What do the NBPTS standards require?
	The standard(s) require the following:
	Meaningful Applications of Knowledge – The accomplished teacher understands how subjects he/she studies can be used to explore important issues in their lives.
	Reflection – The accomplished teacher regularly analyzes, evaluates and strengthens the quality of his/her practice.
	(locate National Board Standards at http://www.nbpts.org)
REFLECTIONS ON LEARNING	**INSERT (describe) THE GROUP'S COLLECTIVE REFLECTION ON WHAT GROUP MEMBERS LEARNED FROM THE EXPERIENCE IN EACH RESPECTIVE LEARNING OBJECTIVE AND THE INSIGHTS GAINED** [Describe what you actually learned FROM the ACTIVITIES IN WHICH YOU PARTICIPATED, and Describe how what you learned is linked to [indicative of] ANY THING called for in the above Institutional Standards
	Learning Objective #1
	To formulate a moral, philosophical problem question, and prepare a brief written introduction to the problem question by contrasting the pros and cons in the problem and by laying out the paper's components.
	Insert reflection here:
	Learning Objective #2
	To use research information effectively to write a literature review
	Insert reflection here:
	Learning Objective #3
	To lay out the structure(s) of arguments
	Insert reflection here:
	Learning Objective #4
	To use ideas from readings as support to justify an ideological and philosophical argument.
	Insert reflection here:
	Learning Objective #5
	To judge how the value judgments in the arguments will help to solve the problem in schools today.
	Insert reflection here:

Developed by Erskine S. Dottin, fall 2004.

BIBLIOGRAPHY

Albee, J. J., & Piveral, J. A. (2003). Management process for defining and monitoring teacher dispositions. *The International Journal of Educational Management*, 17(7), 3463-56.

Arnstine, D. (1967). *Philosophy of education: Learning and schooling*. New York: Harper & Row.

Anderson, E. (2008, fall). Dewey's moral philosophy, *The Stanford Encyclopedia of Philosophy*. Edward N. Zalta (ed.), Retrieved December 29, 2008 from http://plato.stanford.edu/archives/fall2008/entries/dewey-moral/

Auvinen, J., Suominen, T., Leino-Kilpi, H., & Helkama, K. (2004, September). The development of moral judgment during nursing education in Finland. *Nurse Education Today*, 24(7), 538-546.

Baron, J. (1990). Thinking about consequences. *Journal of Moral Education*, 19 (2), 77-87.

Barrell, J. (1991). *Teaching for thoughtfulness: Classroom strategies to enhance intellectual development*. New York: Longman.

Bauer, N. J. (1992). In search of the distinctive contributions of the social foundations of education to the preparation of teachers. *Resources in Education*. Washington, D.C.: Clearinghouse on Teaching and Teacher Education. (ERIC Document Reproduction Service No. ED 353222).

Biesta, G. (2007). Why "what works" won't work: Evidence-based practice and the democratic deficit in educational research. *Educational Theory*, 57(1), 1-22.

Blair, G. M. (n.d.). Groups that work. Retrieved August 3, 2009 from http://www.see.ed.ac.uk/~gerard/Management/art0.html

Blumer, H. (1969). *Symbolic interactionism: Perspectives and method*. Englewood Cliffs, New Jersey: Prentice-Hall.

Breese, L. & Nawrocki-Chabin, R. (2007). The social cognitive perspective in dispositional development. In M, E. Diez and J. Raths (Eds.). *Dispositions in teacher education*. Charlotte, North Carolina: Information Age Publishing, Inc.

Broadbear, J. T. (n.d.). Killing the mook and midriff. Retrieved May 3, 2008 from http://www.collegevalues.org/articles.cfm?id=991&a=1

Burant, T. J., Chubbuck, S. M., and Whipp, J. L. (2007, November/December). Reclaiming the moral in the dispositions debate. *Journal of Teacher Education*, 58(5), 397-411.

Butin, D. W. (2005). *Teaching social foundations of education: Contexts, theories, and issues*. New Jersey: Lawrence Erlbaum Associates, Publishers.

Campbell, J. (n.d.). Theorising habits of mind as a framework for learning. Retrieved October 13, 2008 from http://www.aare.edu.au/06pap/cam06102.pdf

Carver, R. L. & Enfield, R. P. (2006). John Dewey's philosophy of education is alive and well. Retrieved March 2, 2009 from *Education and Culture*, 22(1), 55-67.

Chambliss, J. J. (1987). *Educational theory as a theory of conduct: From Aristotle to Dewey*. New York: SUNY Press.

Collinson, V. (1999, winter). Redefining teacher excellence. *Theory in Practice, 38*(1), 4-11.

Competence and Judgment. (2001). Retrieved on September 27, 2007 from http://www.cogs
.susx.ac.uk/users/bend/doh/reporthtmlnode4.html

Costa, A. & Kallick, B. (Eds.). (2008). *Learning and leading with habits of mind: 16 essential characteristics for success.* Alexandria, VA: Association for Supervision and Curriculum Development.

Costa, A., & Kallick, B. (2000). *Discovering and exploring habits of mind.* Alexandria, VA: Association for Supervision and Curriculum Development.

Coulter, D., Coulter, D., Daniel, M., Decker, E., Essex, P., Naslund, J., Naylor, C., Phelan, A., & Sutherland, G. (2007). A question of judgment: A response to standards for education, competence and professional conduct of educators in British Columbia. *Educational Insights,* 11(3), Retrieved May 1, 2008 from http://www.ccfi.educ.ubc.ca/publication/insights/v11n03/pdfs/coulter.pdf

Council for Social Foundations of Education. (1996). Standards for academic and professional instruction in foundations of education, educational studies, and educational policy studies. Retrieved July 23, 2009 from http://www.uic.edu/educ/csfe/standard.htm

Davis, M. (1992, January). Professional judgment. *Perspectives on the Professions,* 1(2), Retrieved April 29, 2008 from http://ethics.iit.edu/perspective/pers11_2jan92.html

Delattre, E. (1992, January). Professional judgment. *Perspectives on the Professions, 11*(2), Retrieved April 29, 2008 from http://ethics.iit.edu/perspective/pers11_2jan92.html

Dewey, J. (1922). *Human nature and conduct: An introduction to social psychology.* New York: Henry Holt & Company.

Dewey, J. (1933). *How we think: A restatement of the relation of reflective thinking to the educative process.* Boston: Heath.

Dewey, J. (1938a). *Experience and education.* New York: Collier.

Dewey, J. (1938b). *Logic: The theory of inquiry.* New York: Henry Holt & Company.

Dewey, J. (1916/1944). *Democracy and education: An introduction to the philosophy of education.* New York: The Free Press.

Dewey, J. (1960). *Theory of the moral life.* New York: Holt, Rinehart & Winston.

Dewey, J. (2008, January). *Moral principles in education.* Standard Publications, Inc.

Diez, M. E. (2006). Assessing dispositions: Five principles to guide practice. In H. Sockett (Ed.). *Teacher dispositions: Building a teacher education framework of moral standards* (pp. 49-68). Washington, DC: American Association of Colleges for Teacher Education.

Diez, M. E. (2007). Assessing dispositions. In M. E. Diez & J. Raths (Eds.). *Dispositions in teacher education.* Charlotte, North Carolina: Information Age Publishing, Inc.

Diez, M. E. & Raths, J. (Eds.). (2007). *Dispositions in teacher education.* Charlotte, North Carolina: Information Age Publishing, Inc.

Diez, M. E. (2007). Looking back and moving forward: Three tensions in the teacher dispositions discourse. *Journal of Teacher Education,* 58(5), 388-396.

Dottin, E. S. (2009, January). Professional judgment and dispositions in teacher education. *Teaching and Teacher Education,* 25(1), 83-88.

Dottin, E. S. (2006). A Deweyan approach to the development of moral dispositions in professional teacher education communities: Using a conceptual framework. In H. Sockett (Ed.). *Teacher dispositions: Building a teacher education framework of moral standards* (pp. 27-47). Washington, DC: American Association of Colleges for Teacher Education.

Eisner, E. W. (1994). 3rd Edition. *The educational imagination: On the design and evaluation of school programs.* New York: Macmillan.

Epstein, R. M. (2003, spring). Mindful practice in action (II): Cultivating habits of mind. *Families, Systems and Health,* 21(1), 11-17. Retrieved July 27, 2009 from Academic One File. Gale.

Exploratorium Institute for Inquiry. (n.d). *Foundations: Inquiry, thoughts, views and strategies for the K-5 classroom.* Arlington, VA: National Science Foundation.

Facione, P. A., Facione, N. C., & Giancario, C. A. F. (n.d.). Professional judgment and the disposition toward critical thinking. Retrieved May 20, 2005 from http://www.insightassessment .com/pdf_files/ prof_jdgmnt_&_dsp_ct_97_frnch1999.pdf

Fink, L. D. (2003). *Creating significant learning experiences: An integrated approach to designing college courses.* San Francisco, CA: Jossey-Bass.

Freeman, L. (2007). An overview of dispositions in teacher education. In M. E. Diez & J. Raths (Eds.). *Dispositions in teacher education.* (pp. 3-29). Charlotte, North Carolina: Information Age Publishing, Inc.

Fuller, F. F. (1969). Concerns of teachers: A developmental conceptualization. *American Educational Research Journal,* 6(2), 207-226.

Gershman, J. (2005, May 31). 'Disposition' emerges as issue at Brooklyn College. Retrieved April 20, 2008 from http://www2.nysun.com/article/14604

Guilford, J. P. (1967). *The nature of human intelligence.* New York: McGraw-Hill.

Habits of Mind Hub. (n.d.). Retrieved April 5, 2008 from http://www.ansn.edu.au/habits_of_mind _hub

Hansen, D. (Ed.). (2007). *Ethical visions of education: Philosophies in practice.* New York: Teachers College Press.

Hansen, D. (Ed.). (2006). John *Dewey and our educational prospect: A critical engagement with Dewey's Democracy and Education.* Albany, New York: State University of New York Press.

Hansen, D. (2002, autumn). Dewey's conception of an environment for teaching and learning. *Curriculum Inquiry,* 32(3), 267-280.

Hansen, D. (2001). *Exploring the moral heart of teaching: Toward a teacher's creed.* New York: Teachers College Press.

Hattie, J. and Timperley, H. (2007). The power of feedback. *Review of Educational Research,* Vol. 77(1), 81-112.

Inquiry-Based Learning. (n.d.). Retrieved August 7, 2009 from http://virtualinquiry.com/ inquiry/inquiry7.htm

Interstate New Teacher Assessment and Support Consortium. (1992). *Model standards for beginning teacher licensure and development: A resource for state dialogue.* Washington, DC: Council of Chief State School Officers.

Katz, L. G., & Raths, J. D. (1985). Dispositions as goals for teacher education. *Teaching and Teacher Education,* 1, 301-307.

Katz, L. G. (1993). Dispositions: Definitions and implications for early childhood practice. Retrieved April 20, 2008 from http://ceep.crc.uiuc.edu/eecearchive/books/disposit.html

Kelly, D. (n.d.). Do you know what your students are learning? (And do you care?). Retrieved on August 1, 2009 from http://www.aishe.org/readings/2005-1/kelly-Do_you_know_what_your _students_are_learning.html

King, P. M. & Kitchener, K. S. (1994). *Developing reflective judgment*. San Francisco, CA: *Jossey-Bass.*

Knopp, T. Y. & Lee Smith, R. (2005). A brief historical context for dispositions in teacher education. In R. Lee Smith, D. Skarbek and J. Hurst (Eds.). *The passion of teaching: Dispositions in the schools (pp. 1-13)*. Lanham, Maryland: Scarecroweducation.

Koeppen, K. E. & Davison-Jenkins, J. (2007). *Teacher dispositions: Envisioning their role in education*. Lanham, Maryland: Rowman & Littlefield Education.

Kolb Learning Cycle. (n.d.). Retrieved July 29, 2009 from http://www.ldu.leeds .ac.uk/ldu/sddu_multimedia/kolb/static_version.php

Lakoff, G. and Johnson, M. (1980). *Metaphors we live by*. Chicago: The University of Chicago Press.

Langer, E. (1989). *Mindfulness*. Reading, MA: Addison-Wesley.

Leager, C. (2005). Fostering scientific habits of mind. *Iowa Science Teachers Journal*, 32(3), 8-12.

Leo, J. (2005, October 16). Classroom warriors. *U.S. News & World Report*. Retrieved April 20, 2008 from http://www.usnews.com/usnews/opinion/articles/051024/24john.htm

Lee Smith, R. L., Skarbek, D., & Hurst, J. (Eds.). (2005). *The passion of teaching: Dispositions in the schools*. Lanham, Maryland: Scarecroweducation.

Lyutykh, E. (2009). Practicing critical thinking in an educational psychology classroom: Reflections from a cultural-historical perspective. *Educational Studies*, 45(4), 377-391.

Links (2008). Retrieved May 3, 2008 from http://www.habits-of-mind.net/links.htm

Maki, P. (2002, January-February). Developing an assessment plan to learn about student learning. *Journal of Academic Librarianship*, Vol. 28(1-2), 8-13.

Mentkowski, M. & Associates. (2000). *Learning that lasts*. San Francisco, CA: Jossey-Bass.

Miller, H. (2006). Paradigm shift: How higher education is improving learning. Retrieved July 24, 2009 from http://www.hermanmiller.com/MarketFacingTech/hmc/research_summaries/ pdfs/ wp_ LearningParadigm.pdf

Misco, T. & Shively, J. (2007). Making sense of dispositions in teacher education: Arriving at democratic aims and experiences. *Journal of Educational Controversy*, 2(2), summer, Retrieved October 13, 2007 from http://www.wce.wwu.edu/ Resources/CEP/ejournal /v002n002/a012 .shtml

National Council for the Association of Teacher Education. (2002). *Professional standards for the accreditation of schools, colleges, and departments of education*. Washington, DC: NCATE.

Oser, F. K. (1994). Moral perspectives on teaching. In *Review of Research in Education*, 20 (1), Editor, Linda Darling-Hammond, 57-127.

Osguthorpe, R. D. (2008, September/October). On the reasons we want teachers of good dispositions and moral character. *Journal of Teacher Education*, 59(4), 288-299.

Osguthorpe, Richard D. (2007) 'The Scholarship of Educational Foundations: What Does It Imply for Teaching a Course?' The New Educator, 3:2, 103 – 121.

Osterman, K. F. & Kottkamp, R. B. (2004). *Reflective practice for educators: Professional development to improve student learning*. 2nd Edition. Thousand Oaks, CA: Corwin Press.

Peat, B. (2008). Integrating writing and research skills: Development and testing of a rubric to measure student outcomes. *Journal of Public Affairs Education*, 12(3), 295-311.

Perspiration versus Inspiration. (2008, Wednesday, August 20). Retrieved on July 27, 2009 from http://girlprof.blogspot.com/2008/08/perspiration-versus-inspiration.html

Phelan, A. (2001). The death of a child and the birth of practical wisdom. *Studies in Philosophy and Education*, 20(1), 41-55.

Phelan, A. (2005). On discernment: The wisdom of practice and the practice of wisdom in teacher education. In G. Hoban (Ed.), *The missing links in teacher education design: Developing a multi-linked conceptual framework* (pp. 57-73). Dordrecht: Springer.

Pohl, N. F. (1982). Using retrospective pre-ratings to counteract response-shift confounding. *The Journal of Experimental Education*, 50(4), 211-

Professional Dispositions Assessment (PDA) Form. (2006, January 26). Retrieved April 20, 2008 from http://www.aacte.org/Programs/TEAMC/pda_sample_form.pdf

Reynolds, L. T. (1993). *Interactionism: Exposition and critique*. Dix Hills, NY: General Hall.

Ritchhart, R. & Perkins, D. (2008, February). Making thinking visible. *Educational Leadership*, 65(5), 57-63.

Ritchhart, R. (2002). *Intellectual character: What it is, why it matters, and how to get it*. San Francisco, CA: Jossey-Bass.

Rodgers, C. (2002). Defining reflection: Another look at John Dewey and reflective thinking. *Teachers College Record*, 104(4), Retrieved May 1, 2009, from The H. W. Wilson Company/Wilson Web database.

Schon, D. (1987). *Educating the reflective practitioner*. San Francisco: Jossey-Bass.

Schon, D. (1983). *The reflective practitioner: How professionals think in action*. Basic Books.

Schubert, W. H. (2005). Active learning as reflective experience. In D. A. Breault & R. Breault (Eds.). *Experiencing Dewey: Insights for today's classroom*. Indianapolis, IN: Kappa Delta Pi.

Sexton, C.M. (2008). Pre-service teacher dispositions – habits of heart: How do these translate to habits of mind for teaching in a digital world? In C. Crawford et al. (Eds.). Proceedings of Society for Information Technology and Teacher Education International Conference (pp.5318-5325). Chesapeake, VA: AACE.

Shulman, L. (2005). The signature pedagogies of the professions of law, medicine, engineering, and the clergy: Potential lessons for the education of teachers. A speech delivered at the Math Science Partnership (MSP) Workshop, hosted by the National Research Council's Center for Education, February 6-8, 2005, Irvine, California.

Smith, R. L., Sharbek, D., & Hurst, J. (Eds.). (2005). *The passion of teaching: Dispositions in the schools*. Lanham, MD: Scarecroweducation.

Sockett, H. (2009, May/June). Dispositions as virtues: The complexity of the construct. *Journal of Teacher Education*, 60(3), 291-303.

Sockett, H. (Editor). (2006). *Teacher dispositions: Building a teacher education framework of moral standards*. Washington, D.C.: American Association of Colleges for Teacher Education.

Sockett, H. (2006). Character, rules, and relations. In H. Sockett. (Ed.). *Teacher dispositions: Building a teacher education framework of moral standards*. (pp. 9-25). Washington, D.C.: American Association of Colleges for Teacher Education.

Spalding, E. & Wilson, A. (2002). Demystifying reflection: A study of pedagogical strategies that encourage reflective journal writing. *Teachers College Record*, 104(7), Retrieved May 1, 2009, from The H. W. Wilson Company/Wilson Web database.

Spangler, M. M. (1998). *Aristotle on teaching*. Lanham, Maryland: University Press of America.

Spearman, C. E. (1927). *The abilities of man, their nature and measurement*. London: Macmillan.

Stake, R. (1995). *The art of case study research.* Thousand\ Oaks, CA: Sage.

Sternberg, R. (1985). *Beyond IQ: Triarchic theory of human intelligence.* New York: Cambridge University Press.

Stevens, D. D. & Levi, A. J. (2005). *Introduction to rubrics: An assessment tool to save grading time, convey effective feedback and promote student learning.* Sterling, VA: Stylus Press.

Teacher Preparation. (2007). Retrieved April 29, 2008 from http://www.aacte.org/Programs/ TEAMC/teacher_preparation_wsu.pdf Thought-filled Learning Community (n.d.). Retrieved May 17, 2005 from http://www.mtoliveboe.org/sandshore/reportcardwebpages/critthin.pdf

The Conceptual Framework. (n.d.). Retrieved July 23, 2009 from http://education.fiu.edu/downloads/Conceptual%20Framework%2006-19-09.pdf

Tishman, S., & Andrade, A. (n.d.). Thinking dispositions: A review of current theories, practices, and issues. Retrieved 10/25/05 from http://learnweb.harvard.edu/alps/thinking/docs/ Dispositions.htm

Tishman, S., Jay, E., & Perkins, D. N. (1992). Teaching thinking dispositions: From transmission to enculturation. Retrieved 10/25/05 from http://learnweb.harvard.edu/ALPS/thinking/ docs/article2.html

Tozer, S., Henry, A. & Gallegos, B. P. (Eds.). (Forthcoming 2010). *Handbook of research in the social foundations of education.* Routledge.

Tuckman, B. (n.d.). Basic group theory: Tuckman's five stages of group development. Retrieved August 3, 2009 from http://tep.uoregon.edu/resources/crmodel/strategies/basic_group_ theory.html

Valli, L. (Ed.). (1992). *Reflective teacher education: Cases and critiques.* Albany, NY: State University of New York Press.

Van Manen, M, (1991). *The tact of teaching: The meaning of pedagogical thoughtfulness.* Albany, NY: State University of New York Press.

Wasicsko, M. M., Callahan, C. J. & Wirtz, P. (n.d.). Integrating dispositions into the conceptual framework: Four a priori questions. Retrieved May 3, 2008 from http://www.educatordispositions.org/dispositions/four%20a%20priori%20ques-tions.pdf

Wasicsko, M. M. (2007). The perceptual approach to teacher dispositions: The effective teacher as an effective person. In M. E. Diez& J. Raths (Eds.). *Dispositions in teacher education* (pp. 55-91). Charlotte, North Carolina: Information Age Publishing, Inc.

What is Morality? (n.d.). Retrieved August 5, 2009 from http://ethics.tamucc.edu/article.pl?sid= 09/01/20/0751246

Wiggins, G. and McTighe, J. (2005). *Understanding by design* (2nd ed,). Alexandria, VA: ASCD.

Wiggins, G. and McTighe, J. (1998). *Understanding by design.* Alexandria, VA: Association for Supervision and Curriculum Development.

Wilkerson, J. R. and Lang, W. S. (2007). *Assessing teacher dispositions: Five standards-based steps to valid measurement using the DAATS model.* Thousand Oaks, California: Corwin Press.

Wilkerson, J. R. (2005, February). Measuring dispositions with credibility: A multiinstitutional perspective. Paper presented at the annual meeting of the American Association of Colleges for Teacher Education.

Wong, D. (2007). Beyond control and rationality: Dewey, aesthetics, motivation, and educative experiences. *Teachers College Record*, 109(1), Retrieved May 1, 2009, from The H. W. Wilson Company/Wilson Web database.

INDEX

AUTHOR'S BIOGRAPHICAL SKETCH

Erskine S. Dottin received his bachelor's and master's degrees from the University of West Florida, and his doctorate from Miami University of Ohio, and is currently a member of the Department of Educational Leadership and Policy Studies at Florida International University in Miami, Florida.

He won a Fulbright Scholarship in 1988, and served as a Senior Lecturer in social foundations of education at Rivers State University of Science and Technology in Port Harcourt, Nigeria. He won another Fulbright Scholarship in 1992 to serve in Uganda, but declined in order to take a position at Florida International University.

He is a past president of both the Southeast Philosophy of Education Society, and the Council for Social Foundations of Education (formerly the Council of Learned Societies in Education) and served as its representative on the Unit Accreditation Board of the National Council for Accreditation of Teacher Education. He is also a member of the Phi Kappa Phi Scholastic Honor Society.

His research interests are in the areas of humanistic education, the use of case methods and dispositions in teacher education.